Breaking Out
of the Box

Breaking Out of the Box

Adventure-Based Field Instruction

Kelly Ward
Robin Sakina Mama,
Monmouth University

LYCEUM
BOOKS, INC.
Chicago, IL

Published by

LYCEUM BOOKS, INC.
5758 S. Blackstone Ave.
Chicago, Illinois 60637
773+643-1903 (Fax)
773+643-1902 (Phone)
lyceum@lyceumbooks.com
http://www.lyceumbooks.com

10 9 8 7 6 5 4 3 2 1

ISBN 0-925065-96-x

The Library of Congress has cataloged the related text as follows:

Ward, Kelly, LCSW.
    Breaking out of the box : adventure-based field
    instruction / Kelly Ward, Robin Mama
        p. cm
    Includes bibliographical references.
    ISBN 0-925065-92-7
    1. Social service--Field work.   I. Mama, Robin S.
    II. Title
    HV11.W354 200
    361.3--dc22

                                              2005009038

.

Exercises are excerpted from the following with permission:

Rohnke, K. (1984). *Silver bullets*. Beverly, MA: Wilkscraft Creative Printing.

Rohnke, K. (1988). *The bottomless bag*. Dubuque, IA: Kendall/Hunt Publishing Company.

Rohnke, K. (1989) *Cowtails and cobras II*. Dubuque, IA: Kendall/Hunt Publishing Company.

Sikes, S. (1995). *Feeding the zircon gorilla*. Tulsa, OK: Learning unlimited corporation.

*To Bob for his patience, his explanation
of the exercises, and his creativity*

*To Saifuddin, Aziz, and Zahabya for
all your encouragement and support*

*To our students at Monmouth University
in the BSW program who tested the exercises
and the text for us over the years*

Contents

Welcome to Field

This book will probably seem unconventional to you at first. In fact, some of the activities that you will be asked to participate in will not immediately seem relevant, and may even seem strange. We have been trying these activities in our social work field classes for a few years. We have found that students understand the objectives and enjoy learning the points that we try to make in each exercise.

As students, your readings for class will be on a particular topic, such as trust and developing relationships. While you are reading, your teacher is preparing an adventure-based or experiential educational exercise. The exercise relates to your readings, but more importantly relates to events or the process of being in your field internship. The goal of each exercise is to provide you with a different perspective to use in your field placement.

We request that you be open-minded to this teaching method and think "outside the box" – step outside of your comfort zone. If you can do that, most, if not all, of you in this class will have fun using the exercises while learning valuable skills for your practice in social work.

Chapter 1
Getting Started

Orientation to Field

When first entering any field internship, you are certainly hesitant. You know what you would like to happen—a positive and fun learning experience where you finally get to practice your social work skills and knowledge. However, you are nervous and apprehensive about what will really happen. You have probably already interviewed with your supervisor and have some idea of which population the agency serves and what services it provides. Nevertheless, your role and the development of relationships are unknown entities at this point.

Before you begin, take a look at the National Association of Social Workers (NASW) Code of Ethics, specifically the preamble. (The code appears in appendix A.) The preamble provides a foundation for social work practice. It speaks about the mission of social work and our belief in social justice and social change, and clearly describes our core values in social work practice. Each core value has an ethical principle that enhances our understanding of that value.

Value: Service
Ethical Principle: Social workers' primary goal is to help people in need and to address social problems.

Value: Social Justice
Ethical Principle: Social workers challenge social injustice.

Value: Dignity and Worth of the Person
Ethical Principle: Social workers respect the inherent dignity and worth of the person.

Value: Importance of Human Relationships
Ethical Principle: Social workers recognize the central importance of human relationships.

Value: Integrity
Ethical Principle: Social workers behave in a trustworthy manner.

Value: Competence
Ethical Principle: Social workers practice within their areas of competence and develop and enhance their professional expertise.

These core values and ethical principles will guide you over the course of your social work career. They will also help you tremendously as you begin to engage in your field internship. Throughout this book the NASW Code of Ethics will be highlighted and discussed. This is your time to get to know your Code of Ethics well.

Orientation to Your Internship

You have your work cut out for you in the first few weeks, which is primarily your orientation time. Orientation includes time to adjust to the agency, your role, your colleagues, and your clients. Give yourself time to get oriented to the agency and your assignments. Often your supervisor will have you read the agency policy handbook. It may seem boring and a waste of time, but it will be useful later. Any additional training required of new employees is useful as well. Although the odds are that you are not getting paid for your internship, you are expected to perform like an employee. Use the first few weeks of supervision to discuss questions about the agency and your role while an intern. At this point, you are developing a *relationship* with your agency and your supervisor.

In this time of orientation, your goal is to get familiar with your agency's general mission, who it serves, and how it functions. This includes getting to know your supervisor, other employees, and clients. At the same time, you are beginning a new semester at school, getting familiar with the expectations of your professors, and working with fellow students to complete the objectives of this class. It is a challenge to start and develop so many relationships. So how will you approach the task? What will you do first?

Thoughts to ponder

How do you want to present yourself?

- ✔ What is the work ethic you want to present?
- ✔ What is expected in terms of hours and times you need to be present?
- ✔ Is lateness accepted or never tolerated?
- ✔ What is acceptable clothing to wear at the agency?
- ✔ Is there an official dress code?

How does your field internship handle breaks and lunches?

- ✔ Does the agency have them?
- ✔ Are they informal?
- ✔ Do you count the time for your field hours or not?

Do you bring to the internship a skill or prior experience that may help the agency?

The Agency Routine

Early on in your internship you will need to become familiar with the agency's daily routine. How do people speak to each other—do they use first names? How does the day begin—with a team meeting, with coffee? Are there agency rituals you need to be aware of? For example, are birthdays or holidays celebrated?

Why is this important? First, you want to be able to observe how the agency is structured and administered. The atmosphere of the agency envelops its clients, consumers, board members, and staff, and affects the provision of services. Second, you want to become part of the team and find your fit while you are an intern.

Getting Involved in Office Politics

Having said that you should observe and be part of the agency routine, be cautious about office politics. Every office has its politics, and all too often student interns get pulled into them. For the sake of your professional development, you must avoid getting involved in office politics. How do you do this?

Make it a point to talk to everyone. Don't listen to and certainly don't participate in gossip. Be careful about giving advice or opinions regarding staff issues (unless asked specifically by your supervisor). Do your best to stay neutral. Do observe the office politics and learn from them. You can discover many good and bad ways to administer and run an agency just by watching.

Safety in the Field

As you begin your internship, you need to think about your safety while in the field. It is important to preface this discussion with the comment that no disrespect or ill will is thought or intended toward social work clients. Violence in the workplace has increased in recent years, and social workers are not immune to it. Some ideas presented here may seem cold and callous to you. Some of you may be thinking, how could social workers suggest such things about other people? But it is exactly because social workers love to work with people that these safety tips have been developed. The reality is that this world is scary and at times unpredictable. Taking a few safeguards to protect yourself does not mean that you disrespect your clients, or judge them in any way. Rather, you are just preventing potential harm and taking some precautions. These ideas are not meant to scare you from your chosen profession; it is a wonderful and rewarding profession. They should make you think about the situations that you may find yourself in.

Since we live in an uncertain world, your family and friends have probably stressed the importance of safety in all aspects of your life, like parking under a light if you are in a parking lot after dark, not going to an ATM machine at night, and looking in the back of your car before getting into it. All of those common-sense rules still apply, but you need to add one more layer of context to your safety.

Automobiles

When taking your own car into the field, be sure not to leave any confidential material in the car, in case it is stolen. If you are on the way to a home visit, take the file in with you. Use your trunk for any other material that does not need to go into the house with you. Preferably, what you should be taking into the house is the file, note paper, a pen, your cell phone (if you have one), and nothing else, including your purse and coat. Use your judgment about needing a coat if you need to walk far or if it is bitterly cold. More on home visits in a minute.

Find out what your agency expects about driving clients in your personal car. Larger agencies will have agency vehicles and will tell you not to drive clients in your car. Other agencies will have policies that permit taking clients in your car. Find out from the agency about liability insurance (both for accidents and personal injury) when your passenger is a client. Using your car for professional use can add enormous premiums to your personal insurance. However, sometimes the agency policy will cover you during work. Find out and make a decision based on your situation and your individual driving record.

When you are going out in your car for an appointment, with or without a client, make sure someone in your agency knows where you are going and your approximate return time. Keep in touch as plans change, so that someone besides you knows where you are. Carry a cell phone with you if you have one. If you don't have your own cell phone, perhaps the agency has one to use while you're out of the office. Even if you carry a phone, take change or a calling card with you. You never know when you may run out of batteries or be in an area where you can't get a signal. Although pay phones are getting obsolete, they are not impossible to find. Rural social workers may need to use a client or a neighbor's phone; a calling card will come in very handy.

Home Visits

The less your clients need to worry about you, the easier it is to assess their living conditions, which is one of the primary reasons for doing a home visit. Therefore, leave as much as you can in your vehicle and bring in just your necessities. As you don't know what condition the house is in, the less you carry in, the less likely you are to carry out insects or stains from furniture.

Take your lead from the client regarding what room to go in and where to sit. If they don't offer a place, suggest a chair, preferably one with a hard surface, and let them know what you need to accomplish during your visit. Many agencies will require you to go on home visits with a coworker. If there is a policy like that, stick to it and find out the reason it is in place. It could be a very sobering experience to find out why that policy exists.

Wherever you are when working with clients, make sure that you know where your exit is and that no one and no thing is blocking it. This is particularly important when working with decompensating psychiatric patients or those with violent criminal records when they are irritable or agitated. Dress professionally yet comfortably. If you need to move quickly, professional clothes are not as easy to move in as running shoes, but you don't want to be worrying about clothing when you are trying to be safe.

Agency Safety

Just because you are at work does not mean you are completely safe. Know the neighborhood and the neighbors. Let them know who you are. Park your car in a well-lit area if you are going to be at the office at night. If you stay in the office by yourself (not always a good idea), let someone at the agency and a personal friend or family member know your plans. Face it—if you stay late at work on a Friday evening and don't let anyone know where you are, you could not even be missed until you don't show up for work on Monday. Communication is very critical to your safety, both on and off the job.

If your agency has installed some kind of emergency system (e.g., intercoms, panic buttons), find out how and when to use them. The emergency system was installed at great expense for a reason. Hopefully, you will never have to use it, but it would be good to know. Likewise, if the agency offers a nonviolent physical-restraint class, take it. The techniques, especially verbal de-escalation, will come in extremely handy sometime in your career as a social worker or even as a parent!

Like CPR training, safety is a life-saving technique. When you learn it, you say to yourself, I hope I never have to use this. Staying alert is critical to your safety in the field.

Other safety issues

✔ Can you think of areas of concern for you that have not been covered?

✔ Is there information you should know, based on your geographical region, that has not been addressed here?

✔ Can you share other safety hints with the people in your class?

✔ Discuss this issue in supervision and see what safety policies your agency has.

Developing Job Descriptions and Contracts

One of the first things you will need to do with your supervisor is to establish a learning contract for your time in the field internship. This time in field is yours to learn, understand, and integrate ideas into your professional life as a social worker. These ideas about what is expected from you come from your vision, the agency needs, and your professor's assessment of your growth areas. Considering all these factors, establish your goals for the semester. The format for this is usually a job description or learning contract, so that you can be accurately assessed on your progress. For instance, if you have always wanted to conduct an individual counseling session with a client, that would go in your contract. At the same time, your agency has a real need for case management, so that too will go into the contract. Finally, your professor happens to know that you have a real fear of facilitating a group; that too goes into the contract. The contract gives you an understanding of what is expected of you and becomes a working document for supervision and for wise use of your time as an intern. The earlier in the semester you settle your contract, the clearer you will be about how to plan your week.

It is a good idea to read through your field evaluation *before* completing your learning contract, because you can tailor your contract to what you will be evaluated on at the end of the semester (or year). This contract can usually be revised, especially before going into a second semester. Take the learning contract seriously. The more you experience now as an intern, the more competent you will be, and competence will give you confidence when you start out as a paid social worker. Use the worksheets at the end of the chapter to help you think about your learning contract.

Chapter Exercises and Resources

At the end of every chapter there is a short exercise that will help you to reflect on your field placement. Use your imagination to negotiate the twists and bumps in the road of your internship!

You may want to consult internet resources that can provide information related to this chapter. For example, the Massachusetts Chapter of NASW has specific recommendations for safety at work, safety guidelines for social workers, and techniques for defusing or talking down explosive situations.

	Integration of other course material
HBSE	After meeting your first client, can you say what stage of development they are at, according to the theories you learned in human behavior?
Policy	When learning about agency policy, did you find a policy that is beneficial to the client? What about detrimental?
Practice	What social work skills do you use when having your first conversation with a client or supervisor?
Research	Do you have a question about your agency that could be a research project?

Resources

U.S. Occupational Health and Safety Administration
http://www.osha.gov

European Agency on Health and Safety
http://agency.osha.eu.int

International Labor Organization
http://www.ilo.org

Massachusetts Chapter of NASW
http://www.naswma.org

Political Savvy
http://www.politicalsavvy.com

Office Politics
http://www.mapnp.org/library/intrpsnl/off_pltc.htm

 **Begin to develop your learning contract. Answer these questions. Take notes with you when you sit down with your supervisor to discuss your contract.**

What do I want to learn from my internship experience?

What specific knowledge do I want to develop?

What specific skills or techniques do I want to learn or sharpen (e.g., interviewing, assessment, referral, group work)?

Is there an area of social work that I feel I don't have a grasp on or feel that I can't fully integrate (e.g., why policy or research are important to my daily social work practice)?

Do I want to work independently?

Do I want flexibility in hours, or are my days set?

Are there other agency activities I want to be exposed to (e.g., budgeting, administration, board meetings, grant writing)?

What kind of a relationship do I want with my supervisor? My coworkers?

Add other thoughts you have about your internship.

Chapter 2
Building Professional Relationships

For many of you, this may be the first time you are developing a professional relationship. Relationship building takes time, commitment, and work on both ends. In a professional setting such as your field placement, you must develop multilevel relationships with the agency, your colleagues, your supervisor, and your clients.

Now is the time for some self-reflection. Take time to decide how to develop a reputation for yourself. It is too early to determine what theory you will prefer to work from, and possibly what population you will want to work with once you have your degree. However, it is not too early to think about your professional reputation. From the beginning of your fieldwork, others begin to assess you as a professional and watch to see if you are capable of becoming a competent, caring, professional social worker.

Your Relationship with the Agency

Developing a relationship with an entity may seem a little strange. However, it is extremely important. When you applied to be an intern, chances are your application was reviewed by people other than your supervisor. Perhaps a board had to approve your internship, or a volunteer coordinator, or the director of personnel. Individuals within the agency have already begun to form a relationship with you. The longer you stay there, the more your relationships will continue to develop. Other people in the agency will be important for you to know and meet with, in order for you to understand their roles within the agency. These might include the agency president or CEO, active board members, and your supervisor's immediate superior. The more people that know of you and the more you understand their roles, the stronger your relationship with the agency grows.

Never underestimate administrative assistants and secretaries. They often are aware of most of the agency's ongoing projects, and know who is in what meeting, and where and why the meeting is taking place. An administrative assistant who has been at the agency a long time is an invaluable asset. Administrators, including your supervisor, will rely on their assistant for information and assessments regarding interactions with you. You will be able to rely on the administrative assistant for your day-to-day support, like supplies, keys, maintenance reports, and messages. Get to know the assistant quickly!

Getting to know agency relationships

Find the agency's organizational chart. Where is your supervisor in the chain of command? Where does that place you as an intern?

How does your supervisor relate to the other parts of the organization?

How does your agency relate to other agencies in the community?

Has your agency had other interns? What has the history been? What is their idea about interns—how to use them, how to integrate them into the agency?

Your Relationship with Colleagues

By "colleagues," we mean the people who are in your immediate department (i.e., those who you come in contact with regularly). For example, you are an intern in the psychiatric unit at a large hospital. Colleagues would be those people on the unit who share cases with you and work day-to-day cofacilitating groups, or meeting as a treatment team. Although you already have a supervisor, each of these people has a great deal of information about the particular department, and specific skills they were hired for. Watch them interact with clients, and talk to them about their job and why they do it.

These relationships are resources you are developing during your internship; use them to get answers to your questions or advice regarding a particular client or policy. If you develop the relationships properly, you may get hired at your internship. At the very least, you could use your colleagues as references and resources after you leave your internship and start working as a professional in the field.

Thoughts to ponder

What do you need to build a professional reputation?

✔ What is your foundation?

✔ What are the building blocks?

✔ When and how do you add to your reputation?

How much of your reputation comes from your classroom learning? How much comes from you?

One of the challenges to this relationship with colleagues and the one with your supervisor is determining how to keep these relationships professional. In past jobs, you may have become friendly with your coworkers, going out together after work, and sharing intimate details about your life. Although it is tempting, we caution you *not* to start your professional relationships with that type of information. The longer you are at the field placement, the more likely that personal relationships may develop, but remember this is a professional setting and professional relationships are crucial. Learn what you can from your colleagues and keep in mind the professional reputation you are trying to develop. To do this, stick to questions and comments about work, not about music preferences or the latest episode of your favorite television show. Questions and comments about the day's schedule, about clients, and about agency procedure are great places to start. When in doubt, comments about the traffic on the way in or the weather are always safe.

The NASW Code of Ethics specifically addresses relationships with colleagues in several sections of the code. Section 2 is devoted entirely to social workers' ethical responsibilities to colleagues, and covers issues like respect, confidentiality, collaboration, disputes with colleagues, referral for services, sexual relationships, sexual harassment, impairment of colleagues, incompetence of colleagues, and unethical conduct of colleagues.

Your Relationship with Coworkers

Your relationship with coworkers is just as important as other relationships. If you are in an agency where space is at a premium, you may be sharing an office with one or more people. In this situation, clients' confidentiality becomes an issue, as well as negotiating space, having private telephone time to make calls to or about your clients, and giving and receiving feedback from your peers. In order to do this, you need to develop solid relationships with your coworkers. That does not mean that your coworkers need to be your best friends, nor does it mean you have to socialize with them outside of work. What it does mean is that you form a working relationship that allows for space and for support. Each of your colleagues may well have something to offer you in terms of insight and experience, especially if you are just starting in the field.

The NASW Code of Ethics section on ethical responsibilities to colleagues is operable here as well. Review the Code of Ethics regarding your responsibility to coworkers, as well as to the agency and your clients. It very clearly lays out a set of expectations that could safely guide a solid working relationship for you and your colleagues.

Your Relationship with a Supervisor

Your supervisor at the agency can be utilized like your instructor for this course. Your supervisor has agreed to accept an intern for several reasons. Maybe he or she would like to train and guide someone new in the field, or believes that he or she should give supervision because someone in the field helped him or her as a student. Perhaps your supervisor believes that, once you are trained, you will be able to provide more treatment to the agency clients.

It is your responsibility to come to your supervisor prepared with questions regarding the agency, how integration of classroom material will apply to your clients, and referrals and networking. This includes discussing information you need for class assignments, clarity about how to practice a specific skill that needs work, or a request to work on a project or a specific task because of the potential benefit you see in being involved. Supervision is also a time to discuss any issues that you consider roadblocks to successfully completing your field placement. These issues may include transference issues, personal knowledge of the client, or even car trouble or a family illness. As with your colleagues, remember that this is a professional relationship. Questions like "What did you do this weekend?" will not develop that relationship and in fact may harm the professional reputation you are trying to develop.

It is your supervisor's responsibility to assign you tasks and projects as well as to give you feedback on them. Sometimes you will not like the tasks you have been assigned, or will believe them to be busy work. Remember that there is a great deal of paperwork in social work, and ask yourself, if you were not doing this work, who would be? If the answer to the question is your supervisor or another social worker, then it is a social work task that must be completed. If you feel you are not getting the learning experience you expected or that is required for class, you must advocate for yourself. Go back to your learning contract and use it in supervision to discuss your tasks and the commitments made by the agency to your learning. Assertiveness works very well in these situations, not aggressive or passive-aggressive behavior. Assertiveness will be covered in later chapters.

Be prepared to speak with your supervisor every week. Use an agenda to help you organize your thoughts for supervision. We will also discuss this in chapter 10.

The Faculty Liaison

Most social work programs have faculty who serve as a liaison between you and your field agency. Sometimes these people are the same faculty who teach your field seminar class; sometimes they are other faculty in the department. Whoever your faculty liaison is, he or she is an important person to discuss field issues with, especially if you think you are not developing a proper relationship with your agency supervisor, or if you are not being given the opportunities to practice your skills that were agreed upon in the learning contract.

Do not expect that the faculty liaison will solve all your problems for you—you must learn how to do this yourself. Think of your internship as work—if the situation you are concerned about happened when you were employed, what would you do? The first approach is to talk to your supervisor, even if you are having problems with the supervisor! All agencies expect you to follow certain procedures or protocols when you have a problem. The first in line is the supervisor—do not go over his or her head to someone higher in the organizational chart or to the director of the agency until you have spoken with the supervisor. If you and the supervisor cannot resolve your problem, speak with your faculty liaison. At times the faculty liaison might have to mediate between you and your supervisor. This role is part of being a liaison, so be sure to use this resource when the need arises.

The NASW Code of Ethics contains several sections that relate directly to situations involving supervisors and student interns. Section 2.07 prohibits sexual activities with supervisees, students, trainees, or other colleagues. Section 3.01a states that social workers who supervise or consult need to have the necessary knowledge, skill, and competence to do this work. Section 3.01b states that supervisors must be responsible for setting clear, appropriate, and culturally sensitive boundaries, while section 3.01c prohibits dual or multiple relationships with supervisees. Finally, section 3.01d requires that supervision should always be provided in a fair and respectful manner.

Your Relationship with Clients

Client relationships are a little different than the relationship with your supervisor and your colleagues. In this relationship, the client needs your skills and networking abilities, similar to what you need from your supervisor. The client depends on you. This places a client in a vulnerable position, which social workers must respect and protect until the client is no longer dependent. One of your major goals with the clients is to help them become more independent. Then they can move on in their lives, taking the skills you have helped them learn.

You have probably heard many times that if you show warmth, empathy, and genuineness, you will usually be successful in the client's eyes. It is very true and bears repeating here. Take time to consider how to approach your client and how you can assist him or her. Be as forthcoming as possible about what you are able to help with (e.g., you cannot provide housing through your agency, but you can refer him or her somewhere that can). Most people can sense whether you are respectful and will trust you in return. Know when to say, "I don't know the answer to that question." You never want to give the impression that you know more than you do—clients will respect the fact that you can say you don't know. They will want an answer, however, and you must be able to get back to them quickly.

Also remember that your role with clients never changes—you are always their social worker, even if they are no longer a client with your agency. We always tell our students, "Once a client, always a client." You and your client cannot be friends, you cannot use their services (e.g., your client is a roofer and you need a new roof on your house), and most of all, you cannot be lovers.

The NASW Code of Ethics begins with our ethical responsibilities to clients, and includes sixteen very detailed sections. These include our commitment to clients, self-determination, informed consent, competence, cultural competence and social diversity, conflicts of interest, privacy and confidentiality, access to records, sexual relationships, physical contact, sexual harassment, derogatory language, payment for services, clients who lack decision-making capacity, interruption of services, and termination of services. We also have commitments to the broader society, which by default includes our clients. Our ethical commitments here include social welfare, public participation, public emergencies, and social and political action. Go to the code in the appendix and look at all these sections. As a professional social worker you must be well-versed in the Code of Ethics and know how to use it.

Socializing and work

Confidentiality is easy to break, even unintentionally. Be very careful of socializing and talking about work with your colleagues. You never know what a small world it is until you have broken a client's confidentiality outside of work and find out that the waitress is your client's cousin!

Community Resources

Take time to get to know your work environment. The kid who hangs out on the street knows everyone, and one day it may be useful that he knows you or even that you know him. Buy from local merchants, so that they are familiar with your face; it helps reinforce or improve the agency relationships in the community. Agency resources are like your neighbors at home. Hopefully you know them, like them, and can offer some mutual support and aid sometime.

How do you develop these relationships? What are the important elements that one needs for these professional relationships? At the end of this chapter are sample worksheets for you to use in recording contact information or community resources. Use them as you get to know your community.

Elements of Relationship Building

Trust

A basic foundation of developing all these relationships is trust. The agency will not trust you if you do not complete projects on time; your coworkers will not trust you if you talk about them behind their backs; your supervisor will not trust you if you forget to facilitate a group; and your clients will not trust you if you breach their confidentiality. These examples illustrate how trust is diminished, rather than developed. How is it built?

This question brings us back to the professional reputation you would like to develop. Do you want to learn to be a competent social worker and develop the skills you have been taught? When asked to do something, are you so afraid of doing it incorrectly that you express your concerns inappropriately or refuse to complete the task? Your agency, coworkers, supervisor, and clients will be able to sense from your words and actions if they can trust you. Your supervisor will not assign you to a task that you cannot complete. Remember, as you are developing relationships with others, they are doing the same with you. As you are observing them, they are watching you. If you take time to develop the relationship, follow through on all tasks, and communicate clearly and openly, trust will build, and the relationship will grow. As the relationships build, so too will the confidence level of everyone (you, your supervisor, and your clients), providing you with more opportunities to develop your skills.

Dependability

Dependability is another important part of building relationships. Your supervisor and your clients expect that you will do what you tell them you will do. Supervisors expect you to be on time, to be dressed appropriately for your agency, and to call the office if you are going to be late or out sick. If you say you will take on a project or a task, you need to complete it in a timely manner, or ask for help to complete it on time.

Your clients expect you to be on time for home visits and office hours or to call if you cannot keep an appointment. Your clients also expect you to return phone calls in a timely manner. Remember, it is legitimate to tell a client that you do not know the answer to something. You can give him or her the requested information when you research it—but you must remember to follow through with this information. You quickly lose your legitimacy when you do not answer clients' questions, and when you call and cancel their appointments too many times.

Integration of other course material	
HBSE	What aspect of community work are you doing when you are getting to know the people and the businesses around your agency?
Policy	What is the agency policy about relationships at work? What are the consequences of infraction of the policy?
Practice	What is the best way to approach your supervisor about an issue regarding a client?
Research	How could doing research for classes impact your relationship with your clients?

Resources

Social Work Code of Ethics
http://www.socialworkers.org/pubs/code/code.asp

National Occupational Standards
http://www.istc.org.uk/pages/nosunit17.php

International Federation of Social Workers, Ethical Standards
http://www.ifsw.org

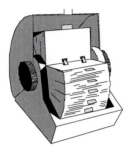

Keep a record of all community and agency resources used and contacts made.

Agency name   **Address**   **Phone**   **Information**

Community Resources Portfolio Template

Agency name

Address

Contact person

Phone

Fax

Web page address

Agency services

Eligibility requirements

Fees

Handicap accessibility

Cultural resources (including languages spoken at agency)

Important information

Chapter 3
Expectations and Stereotypes

This chapter will help you clarify what perceptions you are carrying around with you, as well as what perceptions people may have about you. Before we can do this, we need to define some essential terms: expectation, perception, stereotype, and generalization.

Expectation: to look for with reason or justification (i.e., we expect college students to have good writing skills), to suppose or surmise, anticipate the occurrence or coming of (*Random House College Dictionary,* 1984).

Perception: the psychic impression made by the five senses (sight, sound, smell, taste, and touch), and the way these impressions are interpreted cognitively and emotionally, based on one's life experiences (*Social Work Dictionary,* 4th edition).

Stereotype: preconceived and relatively fixed idea about an individual, group, or social status. These ideas are usually based on superficial characteristics or overgeneralizations of traits observed in some members of the group (*Social Work Dictionary,* 4th edition).

Generalization: the process of forming an idea, judgment, or abstraction about a class of people, things, or events based on limited or particular experiences (*Social Work Dictionary,* 4th edition).

Your Expectations

Let's begin with your expectations. You may not even be aware of how many expectations you have until you start thinking about them. For instance, what are your expectations for this class and your teacher? Spend a few moments jotting these down.

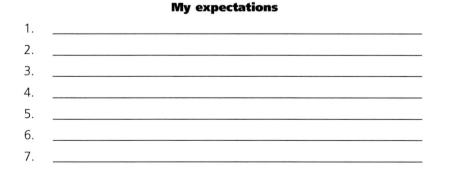

My expectations

1. _____
2. _____
3. _____
4. _____
5. _____
6. _____
7. _____

8. _____

9. _____

10. _____

Does your list include how quickly you expect a response to e-mail or a phone call? What about expectations that you will get an A for the final grade? Do you expect your teacher to be available during office hours?

Are your expectations reasonable? Are they realistic? It is reasonable for your teacher to be available during posted office hours. It may be not reasonable for you to be upset that you e-mailed your teacher Thursday night and had not received a response by Friday morning. If you are a B student, is it reasonable or realistic that you get an A in this class?

What happens when these expectations are not met? How do your perceptions of the class and your perception of the teacher change? Go back to your list of expectations and think about whether they are reasonable and realistic. Do you need to change any of these expectations? Remember, expectations are not goals. They are what we impose on people and/or events. Our perceptions are often what cause the feelings we have when a situation or event is past.

Let's say that you heard from other students that your American history teacher is as old as America and has a monotone voice. What is your expectation? Perhaps that the class will be boring? Are you dreading it? But when you get to class, your teacher has added jokes to the lecture, dresses in costume for the time period that is being taught, and has rewritten the outline for the entire class, making it thoroughly enjoyable. Your expectations of the class made it even better, because your expectations were so low.

Another situation is your graduation day (which should be happening soon after finishing this class!). What are your expectations—sunshine, good weather for picture taking, and lots of space for you to bring your significant other, your parents, maybe your children, or other members of your extended family? But, since nature is in charge of the weather, your graduation day is cold, windy, and rainy. Your grandparents are sick and don't want to come out in the rain. Your expectations were high, so the day may have been ruined. You still graduated, you still received your diploma, but you felt let down and disappointed after graduation.

These two situations exemplify why expectations are so important. Spend some time thinking about what your expectations are for your field placement. What are your expectations of your supervisor? What are your expectations of your clients? Are they reasonable? Are they realistic? Spend a few minutes to answer these questions.

Thoughts to ponder

What are your expectations of your agency?

What are your expectations of your supervisor?

What do you expect of your clients?

Are these expectations realistic?

Are these expectations reasonable?

Field Placement and School Expectations

While you are forming your expectations of the agency, your supervisor, and your clients, they are doing the same of you. Just as your expectations need to be reasonable and realistic, their expectations need to be reasonable and realistic. Some of their expectations will come from their previous experiences with interns, their personnel policies, and the application or résumé you wrote to apply for the internship.

It is reasonable for your supervisor to expect you to follow the agency policy on attendance, and when your day starts and ends. However, it may not be reasonable for your supervisor to suddenly change your hours or require more hours than what is expected for your internship. The agency may have had interns before, and their experiences with these previous interns may have helped them determine what they want from you, or what you will be doing. They may expect you to want the same experience as the previous intern, which may or may not be true. Your supervisor has the right to expect you to come prepared to supervision meetings and the right to expect you will be honest about what you want to learn and how your experience has been thus far. It is unreasonable for him or her to expect you to know everything there is to know about social work and about the specific types of clientele the agency serves, since you are there to learn.

Sharing expectations openly and honestly at this juncture in your field placement is an excellent place to begin building rapport with your supervisor. Let him or her know your expectations of the agency, supervisor, and clients. Ask if your expectations are reasonable and realistic. Ask your supervisor to share his or her expectations of you. Are those expectations reasonable and realistic, based upon your knowledge and experience? Tell your supervisor about your confidence level or concerns about meeting the expectations discussed.

To prepare for this discussion with your supervisor, think about expectations he or she may have about your abilities. Be prepared to explain your knowledge and skills in social work, and with the particular client base the agency serves.

Let's use the same thought process about expectations the school may have about you. By this time the faculty have had many classes with you, providing you with a solid foundation of generalist social work practice. What do they expect from you? As field teachers for many years, we expect that our students represent the university in a professional and mature manner. We don't expect perfection, and we do expect students to make mistakes. We don't expect those mistakes will permanently harm a client or the school's relationship with the agency. We expect knowledge of ethical social work practice, but we don't expect a student to sit around and observe for the entire internship. In the classroom, we expect all our students to come prepared to talk about their internships and bring in cases and questions that have confronted them in the field. We don't expect to answer all the questions, but we do expect effort on the part of our students to listen and to research a topic that they need to have more information on.

Does your teacher have similar expectations? Are these expectations reasonable and realistic? Spend some time with the syllabus from the class and with your teacher to find out what his or her expectations are of you.

These questions may seem trivial to you, and you may think, "Why do I need to even think about who expects what from whom?" We urge you to remember the examples in the beginning of the section. It was expectations that caused the difficulties on graduation day and the opinion you had about the American history teacher. It is important that expectations be clear in all directions and with all parties. Your internship can get unnecessarily convoluted if expectations are not clear, reasonable, and realistic. We urge you to be sure that expectations are addressed in some detail among you, your agency, and your teacher.

Expectations from Clients

Many of our clients who seek services are completely unaware of what agencies can provide, and more importantly what a social worker is and what their responsibilities entail. A recent study (Winston & LeCroy, 2004) asked the general public, "What does a social worker do?" The majority (90%) answered that social workers are responsible for child protection, specifically, taking children away from their homes. Nearly one-fourth of the respondents knew of no other jobs that social workers do. As a soon-to-be graduate, you could come up with at least twenty other jobs social workers do. This is where stereotypes begin to take shape. All over the country in the past few years, social workers have taken criticism for some decisions made by child protective services in various states. (This is a good time to point out that not all state protective services offices require a social work degree when hiring their front-line workers.) Social workers are seen not only as the people who take away children but also as incompetent at doing that job. Stories in almost every state in America report that children have been harmed by a parent or guardian when a child protective services agency was allegedly supervising the home.

Many social workers, especially those who are in child protective services work, are stigmatized as doing a poor job of protecting children. Those stereotypes lead to prejudices that may impact your ability to work with your clients. If your clients have preconceived ideas about you because of news reports, or if their own experiences with other social workers have not been rewarding, you may need to spend a great deal of time building new relationships and breaking down those stereotypes. Hopefully this will not happen frequently, and your clients will look at you as an individual who can help with their situation. You may even be able to develop positive ideas about what social workers do and how they can assist their clients.

Your Intern Status

This is a good time to talk about how to handle the fact that you are a social work intern and not yet a licensed, degreed social worker. It is against the NASW Code of Ethics and probably against the law in your state for you to misrepresent yourself as a social worker, and it was probably never your intention to do so. Section 1.04a of the Code of Ethics addresses this:

Social workers should provide services and represent themselves as competent only within the boundaries of their education, training, license, certification, consultation received, supervised experience, or other relevant professional experience.

Some clients may be uncomfortable working with someone who is not yet a social worker. It is important to be honest with your clients. Assure them you are completing your degree, obtaining valuable training by being an intern, and being supervised by a licensed, degreed professional on the agency staff. Let your clients know that you may not know everything they need off the top of your head, but you will get all the answers for them. Remember, be empathic. How would you feel if you were receiving care from a trainee? How do you feel when you are in a store and get the new clerk who doesn't know what they are doing? Some of us are patient with trainees; others wonder what we did to deserve the new person who is so very slow. Be sensitive and patient if clients are uncomfortable about your status—help them process their concerns with you. Do not hide that you are an intern.

Stereotypes and Generalizations

Stereotypes are negative responses to someone, based on our previous experience or knowledge base. Generalizations are an attempt to lay a foundation about a specific group, so that you have some working knowledge about people; they never apply to everyone in a group. Generalizations should always be checked out before you assume them to be true for the person sitting in front of you.

An example of a stereotype would be that all alcoholics are skid-row bums. An example of a generalization would be that most alcoholics don't seek treatment when their lives have become unmanageable—for some that means a lot of fighting with significant people in their lives, the loss of jobs, or loss of all their money and consequent legal trouble. Do you see the difference?

Think of a specific population and give a generalization and a stereotype for them. Compare your answers with others.

Stereotype or generalization?

Generalization	Stereotype

We all have stereotypes taught to us through our families, the media, and our personal experiences. Be conscious of your stereotypes and make sure that they don't interfere with the services you provide your clients. Conversely, do try to discover the generalizations that exist about a specific population that you have not had experience with in your life. Generalizations can provide very useful information that will make your work with clients faster and more focused for their needs.

Just as you have stereotypes, your clients will have stereotypes about you because of your age, sex, race, ethnicity, and marital status, and because you are a social worker. Take time to answer their questions about you (without revealing too much personal information). Those conversations may make the social work process easier for them and you.

In summary, working with clients is an ongoing process that involves time, continuous effort, and good communication skills, along with good social work technique. Be aware of your expectations, and determine if they are realistic and reasonable. Also be sure that there is open dialogue with your client about your intern status at the agency. Make sure you are clear about the difference between stereotypes and generalizations, and try to disregard and eliminate stereotypes. Make use only of generalizations that apply to the client in front of you.

Integration of other course material	
HBSE	What generalizations and stereotypes do you know about the opposite sex? Label them as stereotypes or generalizations.
Policy	What laws have been passed in America to make sure we don't act on our stereotypes and treat someone unfairly?
Practice	What does a client expect you to do when meeting him or her?
Research	What question could you study to determine what stereotypes clients have about social workers? Or, how would you make generalizations about social workers?

Resources

Public Broadcasting System Global Connections (PBS)
http://www.pbs.org/wgbh/globalconnections/mideast/educators/types/lesson1.html

International Online Training Program on Intractable Conflict
http://www.colorado.edu/conflict/peace/problem/stereoty.htm

Queensland, Australia: Student Health Professionals' Clinical Placement
http://www.health.qld.gov.au/SOP/html/Essentials_Homepage.asp

When did this sign best describe a day in field or in your educational program? What did you do to slow down?

Chapter 4
Getting to Know Yourself, Your Clients, and Colleagues

By now you have begun the tasks you will most likely be assigned for most of your internship, and hopefully you are beginning to feel comfortable with the agency, your supervisor, and your clients. Now is when you will be settling in, and with a little self-reflection, you will realize that you get along better with some people than with others. This may be in part due to your personality and your temperament.

Personality and temperament have been studied for over one hundred years by psychologists, such as Carl Jung and David Keirsey. Personality and temperament tests such as the Myers-Briggs and the Keirsey temperament scale are the most well known of these assessments. In fact, the Myers-Briggs Type Indicator (MBTI) and the Keirsey Temperament Sorter are frequently confused and end up being combined to form one of the hundreds of personality tests that you can find online.

If you spend time looking at the MBTI, you will see that the results describe one of sixteen types. Each type is a combination of four personality traits. Each trait has two options. The first option is whether you are an introvert or an extrovert. Very briefly described, the introvert is someone who reflects and does most processing inwardly. Extroverts do most of their processing with others—they are the people who like to think out loud.

The next matched pair is sensing and intuition. Sensors take in stimuli from all five senses; intuitors follow their instincts or their guts.

The third pair is thinking and feeling. Thinkers like to organize, follow logic, and make objective decisions. Feelers make decisions based on personal interactions and their values.

The final pairing of characteristics is judging and perceiving. Judgers make preferences for a planned, organized life, while perceivers like to live life more spontaneously. The Myers-Briggs typologies are organized around these characteristics, and it is important to note that one type is not better than another.

Keirsey complemented this work by adding another dimension, temperament. He describes four different temperaments: guardian, artisan, idealist, and rational. Guardians are primarily described as hardworking, reliable, and responsible. Artisans are negotiators, and can be resourceful and risk taking. Idealists are energizers; they are authentic and are known to inspire. The rationals are visionary, analytical, and logical. Again, like Myers-Briggs, one temperament is not better than another.

Often these models are combined, and many people do not know the difference between the personality as explained by Myers-Briggs and the temperament as described by Keirsey. Our purpose is not to explain that difference but to help you understand that a lot of information is available from both of these assessments. Most people (notice the generalization) had a hard time remembering their type letters and their temperament description, so a variety of people have used colors to organize the typologies in personality and temperament. In the reorganization, the same four colors are used to describe personality and temperament—blue, gold, orange, and green. Two companies, Matrixx and True Colors, have marketed this organization in workshops designed to help employees work better together.

You will take one of these personality tests to help you gain insight into who you are and how your personality affects your interactions with others. Take time to complete the Color Workshop that your teacher will provide. This personality test, the Color Workshop, was designed by Robert C. Ward of Leadership Bridge, who gave permission to use it here. Contact information is at the end of the chapter. Before beginning, please note that this is not an assessment that you should take home and give your family and friends. Nor is it a workshop to give to your clients or coworkers. The critical part of learning about your personality/color is processing this workshop with your teacher. Specifically significant is the information you will receive about all colors in general, and about how your colors impact you as a social worker.

One last word before you discover your color. Like the personality and temperament assessments, one is not better than the other. You may feel that some words in this exercise are negative; in fact, we all have strengths and weaknesses.

Questions to discuss in class

Now that you have completed the exercise, how do you compare with your classmates?

Are all the colors represented in the classroom?

Is there a majority of one color?

What are the traits that support you in being a good social worker?

What are the traits associated with your color that could hinder your development as a social worker?

What colors do you think may be difficult for you to relate to?

What are the colors to which you will relate well and have similar styles?

Look around the room again at the colors and the people you have done previous group projects with. Are they the colors you expected them to be, based on your experience?

Table 4.1 Color Personality Chart

	Gold **33–50**	**Green** **10–13**	**Blue** **12–15**	**Orange** **12–33**
% of the world				
Good career choices	Business, administrators	Academics	Social work, engineers, organizers	Artists, entrepreneurs
Strengths	Traditional, fulfills expectations	Seeks to understand everything, independent	Morale boosters, imaginative	Learns quickly, troubleshooters
Troublesome areas	Rigid, boring, system-bound	Can appear arrogant or too intellectual	Bleeding heart and too sensitive	Unpredictable, not very serious
Famous people	George Washington, Mother Teresa	Oprah Winfrey, Eleanor Roosevelt	Albert Einstein, Margaret Thatcher	Steven Spielberg, Donald Trump

Source: Adapted from www.Keirsey.com

Please note that although most people in counseling or social work are blue, the authors of this book are gold/green and green/gold. Both of us were social workers before we started teaching, and loved the profession. Our colors did not make us bad social workers, but we approached the profession differently than the majority of other social workers, who are blue. We still consider ourselves to be social workers.

Myers-Briggs trainers do not discuss the skills and traits as strengths and weaknesses, but rather as a mature or immature color or a developed and underdeveloped color. As you meet others who know their color (or you look at the chart with the famous people), you may say, I am not like them; they are so much better at a specific trait. This difference arises because they have developed and matured certain skills that you have not yet had the opportunity to develop. Your skills and traits will develop as well. You also have the skills of your secondary color to fall back on. The challenge is to reach for something that is out of your realm; it is not impossible.

Thoughts to ponder

Look at the characteristics on the sheet that applies to your color.

✔ What are your developed or mature areas?
✔ What are your underdeveloped or immature areas?
✔ Are any areas overdeveloped or dominant?
✔ Are there totally untapped areas that you need to develop?

What Does This Have to Do with Your Field Placement?

Nothing! We just thought this was a fun activity! No, really we have found this to be an invaluable tool in the department of social work where we work, and it has been quite enlightening to students who have recently completed this workshop. It helps explain to many people why they have been able to work with some people better than with others. It also helps explain working styles and how to think about working more effectively with other personality types.

As you enter into your first professional job, you will be exposed to many different personalities that are working toward the same goal. Conflict arises between people because their different personalities work in incompatible ways. Learning to compromise and use every person's developed or mature traits will help your team work better together. When working with others, including your supervisor, it is useful to know how you approach the goals of the agency and what you can offer. You can also ask for assistance from your supervisor to help you with the underdeveloped traits of your personality. Look at your color and be aware of when and how your developed traits can work toward the goals of your agency. Just because your supervisor is your manager doesn't mean that you won't have personality differences. You may be orange and willing to try new techniques with a client, but your supervisor is more cautious. He or she may want to role-play with you to be sure you have all the aspects of the technique, and may want you to be very selective as to which clients you use it with and when you use it.

Remember, we all have secondary colors that we need to enhance. These are the parts of our personality and temperament that need to be more developed—we have these traits, but they are just not as strong as our primary color.

How can you use your color with clients? As you develop rapport with your clients, you will be able to determine what areas the client wants to work on and then develop the treatment plan. Based upon what you know about yourself, you will know in what areas you can easily help clients, and where you will need support. For instance, say you are a gold. If your clients want to be more organized because they can never get a project done on time, you are the perfect person to help strategize options for them. However, if your clients want to be more spontaneous and live on the edge without being anxious about it, you won't be able to help them without support, because you don't see a reason to be spontaneous.

These examples are a tiny fraction of the many interactions that can occur with your coworkers, supervisor, and clients, but we think you can understand the issues that may arise and how they need to be addressed as they come into focus during your internship. Working with people of opposite personalities may take extra time because at first you probably won't be talking the same language, but the time you spend figuring out how to work with one another is well worth the effort. The end result of any project you are working on will be more fulfilling if multiple personalities can see a project through to completion. As this happens, trust develops and relationships grow.

The NASW Code of Ethics contains a section on social workers' ethical responsibilities to colleagues. Section 2.01 deals specifically with the issues of respect.

(a) Social workers should treat colleagues with respect and should represent accurately and fairly the qualifications, views, and obligations of colleagues.

(b) Social workers should avoid unwarranted negative criticism of colleagues in communications with clients or with other professionals. Unwarranted negative criticism may include demeaning comments that refer to colleagues' level of competence or to individuals' attributes such as race, ethnicity, national origin, color, sex, sexual orientation, age, marital status, political belief, religion, and mental or physical disability.

(c) Social workers should cooperate with social work colleagues and with colleagues of other professions when such cooperation serves the well-being of clients.

Developing Your Personality and Professionalism

Now that you know more about your personality and know what is more developed or mature and what is underdeveloped or immature, it is your responsibility to select areas that you need to improve in.

Developing yourself as a professional is an important part of your personality. Your internship is your entrée into the field of social work. You have a unique opportunity to determine how you want to be viewed and what you want your reputation to be as a professional social worker. Are there traits you developed as a student or employee elsewhere that you want to take into your new profession? Conversely, are there traits or habits you want to leave behind? Be aware of what you believe are the characteristics of a good social worker. Which of them do you have? Which do you need to develop?

Your professional self starts to develop here and now, and follows you into graduate work and each and every job. It is your reputation as a professional that will take you from job to job and will develop your career. What do you want people to say about you as a social worker? How do you want to be remembered by former clients?

The History of Social Work

But what is a profession? Why is social work considered a profession? To answer this, let's look at some history. In the *Encyclopedia of Social Work*, Goldstein and Bebe (1995) explain the historical context for the formation of NASW. They talk about the early disagreements among social workers and discuss how each segment of social work wanted to have its own organization. These segments eventually agreed on a set of standards and became one organization in 1955.

Part of the process of developing NASW was knowing what creates a profession. A variety of concepts encompass a profession. The first is the ability to appropriately use the knowledge and skills (techniques and tools) of the profession. A second concept is the qualifications (degree, license, experience) of that profession. The third is establishing and adhering to common values and ethics.

What does that mean to you? Well, as you passed each class toward your degree, you proved that you have the ability to appropriately use the knowledge and skills of social work. You will continue to perfect your tools and techniques and to learn more, but you have met the first criterion. When you graduate, you will have a degree and will need to figure out what license you need in your state. Finally, you have to agree to follow the values and ethics for social work delineated in the Code of Ethics.

Goldstein and Bebe (1995) refer to five other criteria that make a profession a profession, not just a job. These criteria include a theory that is common to everyone in the profession, the authority to act, power to give public sanctions, a code of ethics, and a common culture. The profession of social work meets all these criteria.

Knowing all of that, are you willing to commit to the profession? Do you have concerns about your ability to be a professional social worker?

Integration of other course material	
HBSE	Where do you think personality develops in terms of someone's physical and emotional growth?
Policy	How is policy influenced by the personalities of those constructing it?
Practice	How does your personality reflect and influence how you work with clients and coworkers?
Research	Could your color influence your ability to do research? If so, how?

Resources

National Association of Social Workers (NASW)
http://www.socialworkers.org

Association of Social Work Boards (ASWB)
http://www.aswb.org

Leadership Bridge, creator of the Color Workshop
http://www.leadershipbridge.com

David Keirsey on temperament
http://www.keirsey.com

Matrixx System, National Curriculum and Training Institute
http://www.ncti.org/business/busmatrix.html

Follow Your True Colors
http://www.truecolorscareer.com/quiz.asp

Have you ever come to this sign in your field internship? When, and under what circumstances? Describe what happened and what you did.

Chapter 5
Communication: Building Bridges, Not Walls

What Is Communication?

Communication comes in various forms: verbal (tone, speed, and words) and nonverbal (gestures, postures, facial expressions, and body movements). All communication takes place in a context (the reason for the communication) and in an environment (a room, an office, the street, a subway station, the hospital, etc.). Communication also includes the written word.

When people communicate with each other (other than in writing), they are listening to the words, observing the gestures and other nonverbal behavior, and perceiving the message through the context and environment. All of these factors influence how the message is received, how it is interpreted, and the meaning that is assigned to it. In written communication, the words we choose set a tone (harsh, appreciative, informative, etc.) and lead the reader either to understand our message or to become more confused.

It is very important in social work to be clear in our communications with clients and to think about how to communicate appropriately with them. Communication is one of the main problems that our clients come to see us about. It is at the core of almost every relationship problem that enters our doors.

You have chosen to enter a profession that is very valuable to society. Social work provides services and fulfills a variety of roles within any community. In order to satisfy the roles and understand what we are doing, we have to be able to communicate effectively. Who do we need to communicate with? Our peers in the social work major, the faculty in the classroom, and now our supervisor, coworkers, and most importantly our clients. You will most likely speak differently to each of these groups. Even when topics are similar, the level of communication will be different for each group. So how do you learn to develop a new style of communication with your clients?

First, think again about the type of relationship you would like to develop with your clients. Some of the important concepts include developing trust, making clients feel welcome, using your active listening skills to engage them in conversation, and assisting them with the issue that brought them to your agency.

Examples of communication skills social workers use in interviewing clients

Reflection of feeling: Clarify the client's feelings and encourage further expression of those feelings. "You seem to be angry about the fact that you failed the test even though you studied hard."

Paraphrasing: Express the ideas of the client by putting together the main points and emphasizing what you think the client is saying. "So you are saying that you are overwhelmed by the health issues that your doctor is unsure about, and the fact that your job is not stable due to the economy."

Open-ended questions: Ask a question that can be answered by more than one word. "So how was your vacation? Tell me all about it."

Eye contact: Use your eyes to show clients that you are listening and understanding what they are saying.

Furthering the response: Encourage clients to continue expressing themselves, sometimes with a voice sound like "umm" or "uh-huh" and sometimes with a body gesture that says go ahead.

Communicating with Your Audience

Our relationships with people around us are very dependent on how we communicate with them. Every time we prepare to communicate with another person, whether orally or in written form, we have to first think about who it is we are trying to communicate with. Is it a colleague? Is that colleague a paraprofessional? Is that person new to the field, or someone who is a seasoned professional? Why does this even matter? It matters because you want to engage in a conversation that joins you with people, not one where either party feels intimidated, belittled, or revered in such a way that you can't develop a relationship with them as a human being.

Many professions use specialized language that allows professionals to communicate with each other in an easier and sometimes more efficient way. "Jargon" is the term for this specialized language. A good deal of jargon consists of acronyms, like TANF (Temporary Aid for Needy Families). Some jargon that social workers use you are already aware of, such as "biopsychosocial," "treatment planning," and "summarizing statements." These terms would not come up in conversation with a client but are perfectly acceptable to use with your colleagues. Depending on what agency or population you are working with, there could be agency-specific jargon or population-specific jargon.

Some social work jargon

In drug and alcohol rehabilitation

The rooms	A 12-step meeting like Alcoholics Anonymous
Dirty urine	A urine sample that has traces of drugs or alcohol in it
The hot seat	When someone is the focus of a group session

Hospital work

PRN	As needed
HTN	Hypertension
Dx	Discharge

Board of social services

Section 8	A type of housing that is subsidized through the government
WIC	Women and Infant Children, a program for giving essential foods with appropriate nutritional value to mothers of newborns

Educational settings

IEP	Individual educational plan, similar to a treatment plan and given to every student who has been classified as needing special education (or having a learning disability) and who will receive special services
504 Plan	Result of public law 93–112, section 794, part 504, which provides for special accommodations for a student who has no learning disability but still needs additional services to be successful in school

It will take you a while to learn all of the jargon used in your agency. When you don't understand it, it is completely acceptable to ask what it means. It is the only way to learn. Once you know the jargon, it may take a while to feel comfortable using it, and even longer to use it properly. The common language allows you to communicate across disciplines with colleagues in nursing, criminal justice, and education.

As you use this common language, your communication with your colleagues will improve. It is important to have clear communications with your clients, and so it is *not* a good idea to use jargon with them. The NASW Code of Ethics, section 1.03, provides specific rules on informed consent and how to communicate with clients. These rules cover clients who are not literate, who do not have the capacity to provide informed consent, who receive services involuntarily, and who receive services via electronic media. "Informed consent" is another example of jargon. It means that the client needs to understand what it means to receive social work services and to agree to them, including diagnosis, treatment, follow-up, and research. In order to provide informed consent you must provide clients with full disclosure about who is doing the treatment, risks, alternatives, supervision, and expenses.

Another form of communication is cursing or swearing. It is very commonplace and commonly tolerated (in some places even acceptable). In your professional relationships it is not acceptable to curse or swear. If you curse and swear even occasionally, you must try to refrain from using these words. You may have other colleagues who swear and curse, but it is never, ever acceptable in your work setting. Neither is it acceptable to throw a temper tantrum, act out, or become the office bully. Once again, the NASW Code of Ethics is very clear on this matter. Section 1.12 states,

> Social workers should not use derogatory language in their written or verbal communications to or about clients. Social workers should use accurate and respectful language in all communications to and about clients.

Communicating with Your Clients

So far we have focused on communicating with your colleagues. You must also know your audience when communicating with your clients. What is their age, their cultural background, their gender, and their religion? These factors all affect how you might communicate with your clients, what they will tell you, and how they will talk to you. If you are a traditional-age student and are working with adolescents, you may know their slang or street terms, which will prove useful to you in the long run. It will give you credibility and make conversation easier. However, you may need to ask the adolescent what a word or phrase means if you do not know, just as you ask about jargon. That is OK. The same is true when speaking to elderly people. They may choose words that are no longer used regularly, and you may need to clarify what they mean. You should not use the client's terminology when it is culturally insensitive or rude.

A great deal of information is available on cultural communication. As social workers, we need to be cognizant of the words we use with clients or colleagues and the meaning behind them. Words take on different meanings in many cultures.

We also need to be aware of how communication is carried out with people in a culture that is different from ours. Do you make eye contact? Is it appropriate to shake hands when greeting the client? Who do you speak with first—the father or mother? Under what conditions do you speak with the children? These are all issues to explore with your field teacher and your agency supervisor.

If you are not clear about what you want to say to a client, wait for a moment and gather your thoughts, so you are sure of what to say. Use standard English when you speak. Just as your writing is judged, your speech is judged by others.

When you use incorrect tense or an inappropriate word, people think of you as dumb, ignorant, or uneducated. Most people are reluctant to trust people who appear to not know what they are talking about. You want to sound competent.

That being said, you will use your social work skills to communicate clearly and build relationships with both your colleagues and clients. These skills include active listening, summarizing, clarifying, paraphrasing, open-ended questions, interpretation, and information giving. You will also pay attention to nonverbal behavior, voice tone, voice speed, and eye contact. Practicing all these skills with coworkers, roommates, and family members often will help you get more comfortable with them.

Active listening encompasses all these skills and means that you need to be present in the interview. You can't be thinking about your significant other, what you are going to have for lunch, or the group you need to facilitate later on in the day. Active listening means that you keep your focus on your communication, which will develop your relationship with that specific person.

The Written Word

Earlier we mentioned that written communication is also very important in our work with clients. Later on in this book we will review documentation, but for right now you need to know that how you write has an impact on clients. Choosing the correct words, writing in a logical and clear manner, making sure that your meaning and intent are clear, and of course having good grammar and spelling are essential when you write about or to clients. Because we now rely on fax machines and e-mail for some of our correspondence, we also need to take measures to ensure confidentiality of client information. We must ensure we reply and forward messages correctly and, of course, spell and write in a grammatically correct manner.

Thoughts to ponder

Who will be the hardest person for you to communicate with? Why? What can you do to resolve this issue for yourself?

What is the skill you are having trouble showing competence in? Who can you practice with? What is the best way to practice?

What traditions do you know about for communicating with other people?

How do you ensure that your agency uses fax machines and e-mail correctly?

Integration of other course material	
HBSE	What questions can you ask to determine what stage of Erikson's development your client is in?
Policy	How can we minimize jargon to make the social service system more accessible to clients?
Research	What has research shown to be the traits a social worker needs to have to engage with a client?
Practice	What practice skills do you feel you are already competent in?

Resources

Mind Tools, general business/professional development site
http://www.mindtools.com

Nonverbal Behavior/ Nonverbal Communication Links
http://www3.usal.es/~nonverbal/introduction.htm

 When did you have to "give way" to a supervisor, colleague, client, or fellow student? Without using names, describe each incident, why you "gave way," and whether it was beneficial to you or to the other person.

Supervisor

Colleague

Client

Fellow student

Other

Chapter 6
Insight into Your Client's Perceptions

When working with clients, we use our own skills set to understand where they are coming from and what their perception of the problem is. To demonstrate that, we offer you a case scenario and explain some terms that will help you understand what the client is trying to express to you.

Empathy

Try to go back a few years in your history. Whether you are a traditional student or a nontraditional student, you had to decide what college you wanted to attend and what you wanted to do when you grew up. What process did you go through to choose a school and a major? Did it mean going to look at schools, attending open houses, searching the web, receiving e-mail and regular mail from a zillion schools? Maybe it included conversations with faculty and staff from a variety of majors, conversations with coaches, and of course the admissions office and financial aid. During the application process, you have to write essays, take exams like SATs/ACTs, send records, and get letters of recommendation. Then you have to wait for the acceptance letter. When you are accepted, you go through preplacement testing and scheduling of classes. Just when you think you're done, there is housing, buying books, and finding all of your classrooms. Although it's an exciting time, it's also stressful and frustrating. Trying to get answers, calling people, playing phone tag, and waiting and waiting and waiting are very frustrating.

We remind you of that time because sometimes we forget the details of an experience when it's over. But when you can recall that time of stress, you will more likely treat a freshman wandering around campus with kindness rather than with frustration.

When you treat that freshman with kindness and understanding because you remember your experience, you are treating that freshman with *empathy*. Empathy is putting yourself in someone else's shoes, or as defined by *The Social Work Dictionary* (Barker, 1999, p. 152) it is "the act of perceiving, understanding, experiencing, and responding to the emotional state and ideas of another person." In the case of the freshman, empathy is easy because you actually were one at one time in your life. With clients, empathy may not always be as natural because you may not have experienced what they are going through.

Empathy is different from sympathy. Sympathy is the ability to share and feel the same emotions as your clients. Most often you won't feel the same emotions that your clients do about their situations, but you can always be empathetic.

Let's look at a case and see if you can think of things that this client may be going through, at which time empathy could be an effective tool.

Alice is a twenty-one-year-old single mother of two children, who are four and one year old. Her significant other is the father of the second child and is currently unemployed. Alice is referred to you by her psychiatrist, who is treating her for depression. Alice is also stressed by her financial situation. She tells you that she is working for a retail store as a cashier/stock clerk, making minimum wage and averaging ten hours a week. She lives at her parents' house, but her mother is requesting she leave as soon as possible due to lack of space. Alice's significant other has been emotionally and physically abusive to her, but she believes he will change.

Based on this scenario, list some issues that the client is going through during which she would benefit from the use of empathy.

Issues that you can show empathy about

1. _____
2. _____
3. _____
4. _____
5. _____
6. _____
7. _____
8. _____

Does your list include
fear from significant other?
worry about her living situation?
concern about her financial situation, including paying for her counseling and medication?
resentment toward her mother for asking her to look for another place to live?
frustration about being a single mom of two children?
anxiety about lack of hours and stability at her job?
concern about child care for work and counseling?

What else did you see? All of these issues give you the opportunity to express empathy and give you the ability to develop your relationship. Look at your list again. What are some empathetic responses to some of the emotions you expect your client to have?

Empathetic responses to issues

1. _____
2. _____
3. _____
4. _____
5. _____
6. _____
7. _____
8. _____

Empathy does not imply that you agree or disagree with how the client is managing his or her life. Nor does it mean that you have experienced the same type of situation in your personal life. Rather, it shows the client that you have the capacity to hear and understand his or her feelings. In fact, it is not our job as social workers to agree or disagree with clients' decisions about their lives. Agreeing or disagreeing is judgmental and power-laden. What you would do in a similar situation is not relevant here, because this is not about you. Remember, it is a completely different person who is coping to the best of his or her ability.

Even if you have been in a similar situation, you may have handled the issues differently because of who you are. Often, clients will ask you what you would you do if you were in their situation. When a client asks you what you would do, it is an unintentional trap. Be careful not to enter this trap.

When you answer the question "What would you do if," you answer based on *who you are*, not who clients are. Since your life experiences and your support systems are your own, you will answer this question differently than your clients will. But, it is their lives and how they perceive their choices that matter. Empathy involves staying with clients and supporting them while they make choices and carry them through.

Allow us to detour for a moment on empathy. When the client asks you what you would do, and you have actually experienced a similar situation in your life, this brings up the issue regarding self-disclosure. Self-disclosure means sharing part of your personal life with a client. There are times when it might be useful to share some information about your personal life with a client. However, those situations are few and far between.

Sometimes self-disclosure is useful to build rapport with a client, maybe share what movies you have watched recently, what music you listen to, or even whether you are married. It is not useful to spend much time or go into detail with your clients about your personal life, however, because this could break serious boundaries and set you up for an ethical violation. It would never be appropriate to share with clients that you have experienced a similar situation, and then explain to them how you handled it. For example, it would not be appropriate for you to share with Alice that you have been involved in a domestic-violence situation, or that you are also on antidepressants. However, it may be all right to share the fact that you worked retail at one time and empathize with how it can be frustrating to deal with customers. If you're unclear about the issue of self-disclosure, get your supervisor's and your teachers' input how to empathize with clients while keeping appropriate boundaries.

Let us look again at Alice's situation. You may see very clear decisions for her that will help her resolve some of her problems. Alice could break off the relationship with her abusive significant other, get a job that pays more and guarantees more hours, and force the significant other to pay child support. But what if Alice views the situation differently?

What if Alice thinks she should get a place with her significant other, and have him provide child care while she gets more hours at her current job? You are there to assist her, not to answer questions for her. Ultimately, the decision is hers to make, and she has to implement it and live with what she decides. Your job is to ask questions that help her to feel clear and certain about her decision, and then provide resources and support to make that decision happen.

Your perception of the issues presented and Alice's perception are clearly different. When you are using your reflective listening skills, you should be hearing how the client perceives the situation. When you hear ambiguity and uncertainty, you should ask clarifying questions. If her answers worry you, state that concern in a way that confronts her belief. However, remember that your job as a social worker is to get her to be sure she is OK with her decision and has thought out her options. It is *not* to get her to do what you think is best. Dealing with the client's perception, not your own, makes this process possible.

Letting clients make their own decision makes them responsible for the outcomes and empowers them to be independent. We, as social workers, want both of these elements for our clients. When Alice makes the decision to move in with the abusive significant other, keep the same job, and have her abuser watch the children, you may cringe inside. However, she is exercising her right to self-determination.

Self-Determination

Self-determination is one of the ethical concepts of social work. According to *The Social Work Dictionary* (Barker, 1999, p. 431), self-determination is

> an ethical principle in social work that recognizes the rights and needs of clients to be free to make their own choices and decisions. Inherent in the principle is the requirement for the social worker to help the client know what the resources and choices are and what the consequences of selecting them will be. Usually self-determination also includes helping the client implement the decision made. Self-determination is one of the major factors in the helping relationship.

In the NASW Code of Ethics, client self-determination is an important part of section 1, "Social Workers' Ethical Responsibilities to Clients."

> Social workers respect and promote the right of clients to self-determination and assist clients in their efforts to identify and clarify their goals. Social workers may limit clients' right to self-determination when, in the social workers' professional judgment, clients' actions or potential actions pose a serious, foreseeable, and imminent risk to themselves or others. (section 1.02)

In order to successfully allow Alice self-determination in her case, you have a responsibility to make her aware of her choices and the consequences of those choices. You also have to assist her in finding the resources she needs. In Alice's case, what are the potential consequences of her choices?

Consequences of Alice's choices

Positives	Negatives

What are ways that you, as a social worker, can make Alice aware of the positive and negative consequences of her choices?

Skills and tools used to assist clients to see consequences

1. _____

2. _____

3. _____

4. _____

5. _____

6. _____

7. _____

8. _____

What are the resources you want to link Alice with in order to assist her in making these decisions?

Resources to help clients make decisions

1. _____

2. _____

3. _____

4. _____

5. _____

6. _____

7. _____

8. _____

How would you go about finding other resources for Alice as she implements her choices?

How to find resources and access to resources

1. _____

2. _____

3. _____

4. _____

5. _____

6. _____

7. _____

8. _____

Allowing clients the right to self-determination can sometimes be very difficult. Certainly you don't want to see Alice abused again. However, the best you can do is make sure that she is aware of possible consequences and give her resources to assist her: you cannot stop her from moving in with her significant other. Sometimes, the client will decide that he or she has made the wrong decision. Hopefully, you will have the opportunity to assist the client in making a new decision and implementing that. We say "hopefully" because sometimes the decisions clients make have consequences that prevent them from working on other alternatives. In Alice's case, what if her significant other seriously injures her during a fight? Clearly, that was one of your fears when she told you she wanted to stay with him. But even if you discussed that, you cannot stop it from happening. Other clients' situations could result in homelessness, jail time, or perhaps moving, and you can't help them make a different set of decisions.

How do you handle your client's choice when you think he or she is making the wrong decision? That is a tough question. You must be careful not to pressure the client or degrade his or her choice in any way. "I'll help you get resources," or "I'm there for you if this doesn't work out," or "This will be tough, but we will give it our best shot," are all appropriate things to say. Avoid comments like "I think you are making a poor decision," "You are on your own since you made that choice," or "I never would have chosen that." To learn how to handle this situation, seek supervision about the matter, be sure you have provided all the resources, and wait for the client to make the situation work, or for him or her to come back to you, admit it was a bad decision, and try to change the decision.

Another issue to consider regarding clients' right to self-determination is that often your sessions with clients are limited by outside sources (HMOs or mandated treatment for court-ordered clients). Although you still need to honor the client's right to self-determination, you may need to be more directive and bring up issues in a different manner to assist in the therapeutic process. You still need to build rapport and give clients the right to choose what actions to take, but in a shorter time frame than may be ideal.

Self-Determination from a Human Rights Perspective

Self-determination is a concept that has international implications and is one of the many links between social work and human rights. The concept is present in two major international documents: the International Covenant on Civil and Political Rights (ICCPR; United Nations, 1997) and the African Charter on Human and Peoples' Rights (African Charter; CIAD, 1981).

In the ICCPR, self-determination is found in part 1, article I, which states:

1. All peoples have the right of self-determination. By virtue of that right they freely determine their political status and freely pursue their economic, social, and cultural development.

2. All peoples may, for their own ends, freely dispose of their natural wealth and resources without prejudice to any obligations arising out of international economic co-operation, based upon the principle of mutual benefit, and international law. In no case may a people be deprived of its own means of subsistence.

3. The States Parties to the present Covenant, including those having responsibility for the administration of Non-Self-Governing and Trust Territories, shall promote the realization of the right of self-determination, and shall respect that right, in conformity with the provisions of the Charter of the United Nations.

In the African Charter, the right to self-determination is found in chapter 1, article 20:

1. All peoples shall have the right to existence. They shall have the unquestionable and inalienable right to self-determination. They shall freely determine their political status and shall pursue their economic and social development according to the policy they have freely chosen.

2. Colonized or oppressed peoples shall have the right to free themselves from the bonds of domination by resorting to any means recognized by the international community.

3. All peoples shall have the right to the assistance of the States Parties of the present Charter in their liberation struggle against foreign domination, be it political, economic, or cultural.

Clearly, both of these documents refer to self-determination in regards to the political status of individuals and peoples. However, also contained here is the provision of self-determination in economic, social, and cultural rights, which can include the right to social services, among other basic human rights. Self-determination in human rights is mentioned here to draw your attention to one of the many links between social work and human rights.

Cultural sensitivity and client perception

There is a growing literature in social work on cultural competence or cultural sensitivity with clients. A social worker who works with clients from other racial, ethnic, or religious groups needs to have a special sensitivity to their clients' perceptions of social service provision.

A few issues to consider and discuss are

> ✔ the importance of establishing relationships,
>
> ✔ the importance of knowing your own cultural values, ethics, and norms,
>
> ✔ the importance of learning about other groups, and
>
> ✔ the importance of learning how to sensitively frame questions to clients.

Can you think of other issues?

Using Clients' Strengths

When linking your clients with resources, don't forget one critical resource, the clients, themselves. Ask the client what he or she considers personal strengths. Then point out strengths that you see that the client has not pointed out. Strengths can be internal or external to the client. Sometimes a strength is a personality characteristic like creativity, or being strong-willed or organized. Sometimes it is an external strength like strong family support or financial resources. Using a strengths-based approach helps the client develop the ability to confront weaknesses he or she would otherwise not be able to deal with. The client's strengths are a valuable asset for solving the issues at hand.

Two theories that you will be exposed to in your social work practice rely heavily on the client's strengths: resiliency theory and the strengths perspective. Building on a strong foundation (the client's strengths) gives the social worker time and support to minimize the weaknesses that may never go away. When completing the assessment and when receiving information about the client, remember that you can start working only where the client is, not where you expect him or her to be. This point, starting where the client is, is easier to explain in mathematics. You would not try to teach a first grader algebra when the student has not learned the concept of two-digit addition. With a social work client, you don't want to be numerous steps ahead either.

You may also think in terms of Maslow's hierarchy of needs: from bottom to top, Maslow (1970) lists a human's needs as physiological needs, safety, love, esteem, and self-actualization. Maslow says the needs at the bottom need to be met before you can get to the next level. Therefore, if you have a homeless client, you don't want to be working on self-actualizing. Instead, you want to be providing food and shelter for that client. Find out where clients are, what their thoughts and emotions are about the issue, and be there with them in that spot.

Alice may only be waiting to move in with her significant other to make him happy, so he won't abuse her again. Hear that statement and empathize with her about the situation; don't rush to say that there is nothing to be afraid of, just break up with her significant other. Don't jump steps. Stay with clients and let them go through the process at their own speed.

Johari Window

Named after its inventors Joseph Luft and Harry Ingham, the Johari Window is a way for you to visualize different components of the person who is sitting in front of you, and may help you understand his or her perception a little more clearly. Luft and Ingham's model has four quadrants (windows) that divide people's awareness about themselves into categories.

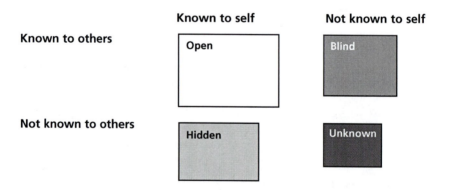

Luft and Ingham believed that we all have information about ourselves that is known to everyone (open), like our names or maybe where we work (Luft, 1970). Then they claimed that there are things that we do not know about ourselves but others see (blind). The third quadrant is what we know about ourselves but is hidden to others (hidden), and the fourth quadrant is what we have not learned about ourselves and others do not know either. Every person will have different-size quadrants because of who they are and what they share. But those quadrants help every person decide what his or her perception is of a certain problem. When we are working with clients, they know two of the four quadrants (open and hidden) about themselves, and you, as the social worker, know two quadrants (open and blind). However, they are not exactly the same quadrants. Depending on how open clients have been and how self-aware they are, they may know substantially more about themselves than you do. They may have a better perception about what they can do or what to act upon. As a social worker, you are working on getting the client to have a large open quadrant and very small blind and unknown quadrants.

Pick someone else in the class who knows you fairly well. Spend some time filling out your own Johari window in the open area and then spend some time thinking about the blind area of your partner. Compare notes on those two areas. Did your partner know what you considered to be open information? Did your partner know the things you considered blind?

Comparing quadrants

Your open area	Your partner's blind area

Thoughts to ponder

How would you go about creating a larger open area in your Johari window?

Is having a large open area appealing to you?

How do you figure out what is in your unknown area?

Integration of other course material	
HBSE	What does stage of development have to do with how clients perceive the world?
Policy	When is a client's right to self-determination not the priority?
Practice	Do you have suggestions on what social work techniques can help someone decide what is known to others and not known to self?
Research	How does your client's perception impact the single system design research model?

Resources

Johari Window, Augsberg College
http://www.augsburg.edu/education/edc210/johari.html

Mental Health Network on empathy
http://mentalhelp.net/psyhelp/chap13/chap13c.htm

Self-determination
http://www2.plattsburgh.edu/acadvp/libinfo/library/er/swk308r22.pdf

Abraham Maslow
http://web.utk.edu/~gwynne/maslow.htm

African Charter on Human and People's Rights
http://www.hrcr.org/docs/Banjul/afrhr.html

International Covenant on Civil and Political Rights
http://www.hrweb.org/legal/cpr.html

What can you do independently at your intership and what do you have to ask permission to do? Describe both situations and how they make you feel.

Chapter 7
Put It in Writing!

When we talked to social work students about why they want to be social workers, no one ever told us that it was because they love to write or that they heard social work documentation was fun! Believe it or not, social work documentation doesn't even rank in the top ten reasons to become a social worker. Yet documentation is a vital component of every social work job. Social work documentation comes in a variety of styles and has many purposes. Each agency that employs you will have its unique form of documentation, which depends on the state regulations and accrediting bodies that oversee the services that the agency provides.

What we want to discuss here are the most common types of social work writing—what they are, what context you might use them in—and how to improve your writing skills. We will cover progress notes, psychosocials, process recordings, treatment plans, quarterly reports, grant writing, statistical reports, and writing for publication. In covering these areas we will discuss good writing skills, writing styles, and plagiarism.

Progress Notes

One important lesson about documentation that you will hear over and over again in your career is this: *if it isn't written, it never happened.*

If a client of yours who was laid off from his job goes to his old place of employment, kills his former boss and coworkers, and then kills himself, there is bound to be an investigation. Who has access to those records during the investigation is another subject, but definitely your supervisor, the agency director, and perhaps an agency lawyer are going to look at those files. If you did not write in your notes that your client denied suicidal and homicidal ideation, you and your agency could be held responsible for all the deaths, because the proper documentation is not in place. That is not something you want to go through, so remember: document ... document ... document! If it is not in writing, it did not happen!

You need to keep accurate records of any action about a client that occurred when you were involved. This includes phone conversations, any correspondence about or with the client, and notes from contacts and sessions with your client. If you called to cancel a meeting with a client, you should write the date, time, and what happened (e.g., talked to the client, no answer, busy, left message on an answering machine or with a person). If you receive messages from a client, through a receptionist, in writing, or on voice mail, you may transfer that information into a case file or keep the message in a separate section of the file.

Believe it or not, most times it's easier to do both, because little notes get lost, but it is always helpful to have the original.

Progress notes come in many different formats, and you should determine what format your agency uses. During the course of your career you may learn many formats. Some formats that the authors are familiar with include

SOAP: subjective information, objective information, assessment and conclusion, plan

DAP: data, assessment, plan

POT: problem, orientation, treatment plan

POR: problem-oriented record

Now there are jargon and acronyms for you, as discussed in chapter 5!

Each of these types of documentation captures similar content. Find out as soon as you start at an agency what format the agency uses. The same information documented two different ways, in SOAP and in DAP, might look like this:

July 20, 2006

S: Client came in for initial session appearing disheveled and tired.

O: Social worker completed intake and addressed appearance, finding that the client has been living in his car since being evicted from his house for not paying rent.

A: Client is in need of housing.

P: Refer client to local emergency housing after confirming eligibility and availability; provide client with transportation.

Kelly Ward, PhD, LCSW, CADC (actual signature)

July 20, 2006

D: Client states he has been evicted and is now homeless when he enters the agency for his intake assessment.

A: Client feels worried that he has no place to live as well as embarrassed that he is seeking assistance.

P: Refer client to local emergency housing after confirming eligibility and availability; provide client with transportation. Help client feel comfortable with needing to accept assistance.

Kelly Ward, PhD, LCSW, CADC (actual signature)

Observe that basically the same information is in both types of documentation. Notice that the plan is exactly the same at first, but because you know the client's feelings, you can add a piece that assists the client with his feelings about needing help.

Larger institutions and agencies will have a documentation preference. If you go to a smaller agency or a place that is just adding a social work component to a program, they may not have a procedure in place. At that point, you should discuss the options with your supervisor and check with funding sources and your licensing bodies to see what they suggest. In private practice, you may choose the documentation format that works for you—but be sure to document.

Psychosocials

Psychosocials, sometimes called biopsychosocials or initial assessments, are typically created when a new client comes to your office. As in the case of progress notes, most agencies have their own biopsychosocial forms that contain relevant information for that agency.

Our first suggestion when filling out the form is to remember that the initial goal is to get to know the client and make him or her feel comfortable, not to fill out the form. If you can, read any information that the agency has on this client, especially demographics like gender, date of birth (DOB), and address. If the agency has this information, all you need to do is verify it with the client. Implementing this process in the initial session lets the client know that he or she doesn't have to repeat similar information for the umpteenth time, and it allows you to start with simple questions to ease the anxiety you and your client may be experiencing.

The rest of the information on a biopsychosocial assessment is usually grouped by related questions that allow you to get the information in a conversational ways, as you would with someone you are simply trying to get to know. In other words, try to group the questions by similar subjects, but ask them in an order that you think will allow the client to feel most comfortable. When asking these questions, you will begin to use all the questioning techniques that you have learned: open-ended questions, probing questions, clarifying questions, and so on. Try to get an accurate picture of a client's life, how history and the current environment have aided or deterred the client in the current situation, and why the client is presenting to your agency for services at this time.

It is wise before you begin the psychosocial to introduce yourself and to let the client know what you are doing, how long it will take, and who will get to see the information. A standard introduction may go something like this:

> Hello. Mrs. Hughes, my name is Robin Mama, and I am a social work intern here at ABC agency. I need to make sure all of the entrance paper work is completed before we continue. Is that OK with you? It will take us about 45 minutes and will give me a good understanding of how we can best help you. Everything you tell me is confidential unless you tell me you are going to harm yourself or anyone else. Are there any questions? If not, let's begin. If you don't mind, I will take a few brief notes during our conversation.

This helps your client to understand the process. It also lets him or her know that you might take some notes during the interview. One word of caution here: don't get so caught up in taking notes that you do not listen to or keep eye contact with your client! The client might think you are being rude, and you are—note-taking is to be used judiciously, *not* throughout the whole interview. You must attend to the client when he or she is speaking. If the client becomes emotional in any way, you must put down your pen or pencil and stop writing.

Let's discuss some of the questions that usually appear on psychosocials. Sometimes you will look at the questions and say, "That is not relevant to this client, I won't ask that question." For instance, sexual activity and sexual orientation are often questions on a psychosocial. Perhaps you have a seventy-five-year-old widow sitting in front of you and you think, "Oh, she doesn't have sex." How do you know? Perhaps her next door neighbor is a widower and they have been having sex regularly.

Often questions about drug and alcohol consumption are on psychosocials. If you are sitting with a child, you might think you don't have to ask these questions. Well, if you talked to drug/alcohol specialists, they could tell you horror stories of children being high or drunk as young as age eight or nine. You could use these questions to widen the scope of the interview by asking if anyone in their family uses drugs or alcohol and to probe for other important information. Don't overlook opportunities to get more information than the question is calling for.

Another often overlooked question is military history. Again, many people will overlook this when interviewing children. Their parents may have been in the military, however, or have been killed in action. Maybe the child has never lived in one place for long, because the family was reassigned frequently.

Work history is another overlooked part of psychosocials. Anyone working in occupational safety and health will tell you that getting a detailed work history is often essential for medical reasons. Many of the substances or chemicals that people work with can cause severe medical problems or diseases. One has only to look at the experiences of workers who were exposed to asbestos to see how devastating this can be. In the case of asbestos exposure, not only did workers develop lung disease, but their wives often developed lung cancer from washing their husbands' clothes.

Two last suggestions about psychosocials—don't assume ethnicity or gender from your observation. You don't want someone who is transvestite (cross dresser) or transgendered (had a sex change) to not tell you his or her true identity because you assumed the person in front of you was female. Also, don't assume that because a person has dark brown skin that he or she is African American. Be culturally sensitive and ask for ethnicity or racial background.

While doing the biopsychosocial is the perfect time to complete a genogram and ecomap of the client's life. Some agencies have separate forms for you to fill out; if not, just take blank paper or the back of the biopsychosocial and start to draw. If you have not yet learned how to do a genogram or ecomap, take time to learn. Both give an excellent one-page view of the client's life history, highlighting family patterns, relationships, and current connections to other areas of his or her system. Look in appendix B for a psychosocials format designed by Nora Smith and Irene Bush of Monmouth University, (used by permission).

Figure 7.1

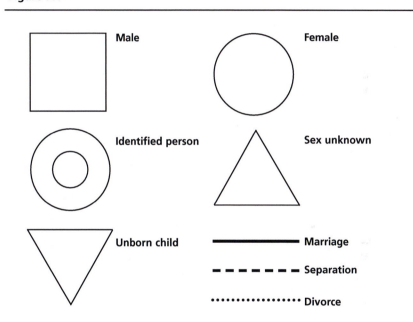

Constructing genograms and ecomaps

Figure 7.1 shows the symbols used in making genograms and ecomaps. We put these symbols together to form relationships, to indicate how people are related, and to determine what common issues they share. Present at least three generations of a family, including all marriages, divorces, children and pregnancies, ethnicity, and religion. Also include physical location(s) of people in the family, and who lives with whom.

If you remember that the form in front of you is not the focus, and that developing a relationship with the client in order to assist them is the goal, then you will do fine. Eventually, when you have been working in an agency for a while, you will be able to remember most of the form and what the client says without writing it down until after the interview.

We need to say a word here about client access to records. Every agency has a policy on whether clients can access their records and, if so, how a client can do this. Section 1.08 of the NASW Code of Ethics contains specific information about client access to records, when this should and should not be available, concerns leading to protection of client confidentiality. Read the code and ask your agency about this policy.

In addition, section 3.04 of the Code of Ethics specifies that documentation should be accurate, meet deadlines, protect clients' privacy rights, and be stored once services are terminated.

Treatment Planning

Treatment planning will be covered in greater depth in a later chapter, but needs to be mentioned here. Treatment plans are not written as frequently as progress notes, but the treatment plan is the backbone of every progress note you write. The treatment plan is like your road map to get to the end of treatment. When the client has accomplished all treatment goals, then they have successfully completed treatment. The treatment plan is developed from the initial assessment. Usually the agency will have subareas in the treatment plan for health, education, employment, relationships, and legal issues. Treatment plans are the legal contract between you and the client. They usually include goals and objectives, names or positions of the responsible parties, target dates, and signatures of all involved in the treatment plan. Be aware that this is a legally binding document and must be adhered to in terms of goals, objectives, and target dates. A sample of a treatment plan appears in chapter 9.

Quarterly Reports

Depending on how long your clients are in your program, you may need to write quarterly reports. If the program is long-term (six months or longer), you will write a report every three months to summarize the quarter, while addressing progress or lack of progress on the client's treatment goals. Quarterly reports may also be requested from referral sources, so that they are kept abreast of the client's status in your program.

Quarterly reports are usually formatted to look like a narrative of each treatment goal in the same order that the treatment plan is written. It is common for the strengths and successes to be noted first, followed by the areas where continued treatment is recommended. Each agency will probably have its own format or form for you to use, so check to see if a format is in place. Here is an example of a quarterly report format.

Quarterly Report for [Client's Name]

Goal one. Client's strengths and completed tasks are written first, followed by areas that need continued work, usually in a second paragraph: Client has a goal to remain drug and alcohol free. During the first quarter of his treatment, the client has submitted urines that have tested negative and has received a 90-day key chain from NA (Narcotics Anonymous). Staff continues to see positive changes in his behavior. He has increased insight into how drug use had impacted his life up until entry to the program 3 months ago.

Goal two. Continue same format, listing positive steps first, followed by areas that need work, such as: Although client remains free of drug and alcohol, he has not yet obtained employment. Client's previous employment was always related to drug dealing (runner, mule, or look out). Due to client's lack of high school diploma and no work experience, the client is struggling. Client has agreed to enroll in adult education to work toward obtaining his GED and test for vocational aptitude.

Goal three. Follow same format.

Summary statement. Summarize how much work has been done, what needs to be done, and recommendations that need to be considered.

Other Documentation

Other documentation related to direct service for clients might include letters to court if the client has legal difficulty, and written requests to other agencies for assistance (furniture, payment of utilities, or request for a legal document). In any event, other forms of documentation for the client are not as common or frequent as progress notes, psychosocials, treatment plans, or quarterly reports, so we just want to make you aware that they exist. When and if you have other direct services documentation, it is best to consult with your supervisor about format, expectations, and appropriate style (e.g., letters to court are always very formal, with proper titles and salutations for judges).

Depending on the type of agency you work in, there is bound to be other direct care documentation. For instance, residential facilities commonly have a journal where staff document the events that occurred during that shift. Although in most places the writing style is very informal (just to bring all staff up-to-date), it is still a legal record and your signature denotes that what you stated is fact. Usually there is also an incident report to document a serious injury or infraction of the program rules, which goes to the agency administration and into the client's files. Incident reports generally are just facts, not observations or opinions.

There may also be a medication log if staff dispense medication. Make sure you are trained and feel comfortable dispensing medication if your agency requires it.

Many of the forms and information you process are time-sensitive, so you need to be very aware of reporting deadlines. In some agencies, intakes or initial assessments might need to be completed within 36–48 hours. For child protective services agencies, the turn-around time is much faster. Check deadlines with your supervisor and be sure to allocate time during your day to complete your documentation.

Administrative Writings

Thus far, we have dealt with documentation that is primarily related to the client and client services. However, many of you may be working in a macro approach to social work and will have little or no contact with clients; much more writing will be entailed in your job description. Sometimes, even when you prefer direct practice, you are given a supervisory role in which you will be expected to prepare administrative documents.

Many administrators or supervisors prepare quarterly reports. These reports are usually summaries of the entire program that are sent to the program director/president or a funding source. Formatting of this quarterly report is similar to the direct service quarterly report about the client. You will write the report, following the program goals and objectives and listing strengths and weaknesses, and attaching any supporting documentation in an appendix. Sometimes, if you are lucky, the funding agency has a format/form they want you to use, and you can better provide exactly what they want.

Grant Writing

Social work agencies receive funds from various sources. Many agencies rely on grants to fund the services and programs that they provide. Grant money is used to start programs, to fund programs already in place, or to evaluate programs. Some grants are renewable, while others are for a specific time period. Each grant has specific provisions for reporting to the grant source about the program. Sometimes this involves monthly reports, sometimes quarterly or biannual reports, and always a final report. These reports have to be written as specified in the grant. This is not the place to teach you how to write grants. Helpful resources are found at the end of this chapter.

Student Writing

When you meet your supervisor for supervision, he or she needs to understand what interactions occurred between you and your clients. If your supervisor is present to watch that interaction, you or your client may act unnatural and your supervisor cannot really observe your skills with much accuracy. In an effort to minimize this problem, process recording was developed. Before audio- and videotaping and one-way mirrors, the only way to observe the interaction was for the social worker to write it down verbatim. In a column next to the conversation, social workers wrote down their thought process. A third column allowed the supervisor to make comments to the social worker. Process recording is an invaluable tool for growth and understanding how you are interacting and communicating with clients. We have heard many social workers who have been in the field for years say that, when they are really stuck, process recording is still the best way for them to understand what is happening in their interaction with the client and what their gut feelings are about that interaction. Appendix C has two examples of process recording sheets.

Writing Style

As a student you have been maturing as a writer and may be accustomed to writing in one style. As you can see by what we have discussed, your writing style is about to change. You will need to figure out the appropriate style for what you are writing. As already stated, grants, quarterly reports, and court letters are very professional. Treatment plans are rarely ever narrative and can sound a bit choppy, but they are essentially an outline. Progress notes are short and decisive, whereas logbooks are often fairly informal. Know your audience, and know what is expected with your writing. You may at some point decide that you would like to write for publication. Take a look at articles in your social work journals to see how they are written. Each journal has a particular focus and style— you will need to follow that style if you want your article to be considered for publication.

We have written this book intentionally in a colloquial voice. This is because it is informal and contains fun activities designed for a field class, which is really about discussion. If this book were a policy book or a research book, it would be written in a different style.

You have been writing term papers that require a particular style. The preferred style for social work is usually the American Psychological Association format (APA). Some disciplines follow the Chicago manuscript style. Please make sure you are aware of the requirements for documenting and completing a bibliography. The styles are very precise and exact. If you ever write for publication, your manuscript will not be read if it is in the wrong format. Spend time learning the correct format because it will benefit you through grad school and into your professional career. Try hard not to mix formats. This is a common and easy mistake when you are accustomed to one way of writing and then get asked to switch styles.

Regardless of what you are writing, use correct spelling and grammar. When people don't meet you, one of the things they judge you by is the quality of your writing. Don't allow people to think you are unqualified to be a social worker. If your writing skills needs improvement, work on them now while in school. Check to see if your school has a writing center or inexpensive tutors who can proof your work and give you a few pointers. Also, don't rely on spell-check programs in your word-processing programs. Many typing errors won't get picked up by a spell-check.

Writing in social work takes on many dimensions. Find out what is expected and get help if you need it. It can be complicated, confusing, and overwhelming, but stay on top of your documentation and you will be fine.

Plagiarism

One last word about writing. Know what plagiarism is and what it is not. Plagiarism is the use of someone else's work without giving him or her credit for the work. It is illegal and unethical, causing students to fail and ruining careers. Whenever you see an idea in print or on the internet or hear it in a speech, and you think it will be useful information to your work, give credit to the author/speaker. The APA stylebook gives you an entire chapter on how to cite almost anything. Inadequate referencing is almost as bad as plagiarism, and many consider the two to be equivalent.

The NASW Code of Ethics in section 4.08 spells out your responsibility to give credit.

> (a) Social workers should take responsibility and credit, including authorship credit, only for work they have actually performed and to which they have contributed.

> (b) Social workers should honestly acknowledge the work of and the contributions made by others.

Thoughts to ponder

What are my writing strengths? What areas can I work on now?

What do I feel about process recordings? How can I make it easier for myself to remember the conversation that I will use in a process recording?

What do I understand about plagiarism, and how can I avoid it?

Integration of other course material	
HBSE	What is the best way to document history of genetic health problems, mental illness in family, and substance abuse in order to see patterns developing?
Policy	What are the legal implications if you have documented improperly or have forgotten to document?
Practice	How can your documentation help you enhance your social work practice?
Research	When reading an article on a research study, how can you tell where the authors based their study and why?

Resources

APA style
http://www.referencepointsoftware.com
http://webster.commnet.edu/apa
http://owl.english.purdue.edu/handouts/research/r_apa.html

Chicago style
http://library.osu.edu/sites/guideschicagogd.html
http://www.libs.uga.edu/ref/chicago.html

Grant writing
http://grants.nih.gov/grants/grant_tips.htm
http://www.fdncenter.org
http://www.npguides.org

What first comes to mind when you see this street sign? How would you relate this to your field internship?

Chapter 8
Pick a Theory, Any Theory

Social work is a profession that you can be proud to be joining shortly. Do you remember learning about Dr. Alexander Flexner in your social welfare history class? Flexner addressed the 1915 conference on charities and corrections and flatly told the social work audience that social work was not a profession. The established professions (law, medicine, and religion) had three criteria for becoming a profession: a body of knowledge used to practice from, specific and defined skills, and ethics. The definition of a profession did not include using a common theory.

At one time the counseling profession as a whole (social workers, psychology, and counselors) selected a theory that they focused on, and clients sought them out because they were cognitive behavioralist or psychoanalytic theory experts. Now the profession has recognized that one-size theories do not fit all people (both clients and social workers), and there should be options to choose from when practicing and doing research. There are so many frameworks to choose from that you will never be expected to know and perfect each one. So we will present the theories in categories, emphasizing what we see as some of the main ideas, goals, techniques, social worker's role, and how the theoretical framework you choose makes the work you do different for each case.

You probably want to talk to your supervisor about social work theories during your next supervision session. Often agencies like drug and alcohol treatment centers, rehabilitation programs, schools, residential treatment centers, and detention centers choose a theory and model for their entire program. The entire program will be built around that theory, frequently some type of behavioral program. You do not want to be practicing from a theory contrary to what they are using, because it will confuse clients and delay the results you are trying to achieve.

Although some theories work better for some populations (e.g., behavior modification works well with children), one theory is not necessarily better than the another. Many theories have their own nuances that you will perfect with training and practice. Based on your personality, values, and skills, you will probably prefer one theoretical framework over the others. That is fine. Just don't limit your practice as a social worker to one theory, because every client will not respond to every theory.

When you discuss theory with experienced social workers, they often do not know what theory they practice, unless of course they work for an agency that has selected a theoretical framework. Sometimes the social worker doesn't know the name of the theory because he or she has adopted an "eclectic style," choosing techniques and ideas from a variety of theories and using what works for him or her and the client, rather than being a purist and adhering to one theory. Know what skills come from what theory and know why you choose particular skills and techniques.

The NASW Code of Ethics does not speak directly to the issue of what social work theory you should work from; however, the code does speak to the competence of the social worker in section 1.04.

(a) Social workers should provide services and represent themselves as competent only within the boundaries of their education, training, license, certification, consultation received, supervised experience, or other relevant professional experience.

(b) Social workers should provide services in substantive areas or use intervention techniques or approaches that are new to them only after engaging in appropriate study, training, consultation, and supervision from people who are competent in those interventions or techniques.

(c) When generally recognized standards do not exist with respect to an emerging area of practice, social workers should exercise careful judgment and take responsible steps (including appropriate education, research, training, consultation, and supervision) to ensure the competence of their work and to protect clients from harm.

Before introducing the theory groupings, we present a client case. This case will be used to demonstrate the different theories and how they can be used, in general terms. To go into specifics about the nuances of a case and how to apply the theory would take almost as long as writing about each and every theory. So our plan is to introduce an abbreviated version of the case and show how to apply the basic ideas and techniques to the case.

Darlene

Darlene is a sixteen-year-old Caucasian girl who is the adopted and only child of an intact family (social work jargon for parents who are still together). She lives in a middle-class suburb that her parents chose specifically because of the school system's reputation for excellent education and a high college acceptance rate. Mom and Dad are both educated professional people. Darlene has no interest in school, breaks every rule she possibly can, and has done so since eighth grade. The principal of her junior high almost didn't pass her because of excessive detentions and low grades. Darlene is in counseling because she was arrested for shoplifting and her probation requires counseling.

When you meet Darlene, she admits to smoking cigarettes and sneaking alcohol regularly from her parents' extensive liquor cabinet. She has used marijuana, and is considering trying ecstasy and sniffing glue. Her first sexual experience was at fifteen when her parents took her on vacation. She sneaked out of the cabin when they were asleep. A "thirty-something"–year-old man bought her alcohol in exchange for sex. She doesn't want to talk about it, but says she is sure he thought she was twenty-one because that is what she told him.

Darlene dislikes school, has mostly Cs and Ds, and has no desire to go to college. She is almost always in trouble for truancy or falling asleep in class. In freshman year, her class went on a field trip to a local drug rehabilitation center to deter drug use. Darlene thought it was "cool" and that it would not be so bad if she had to go there one day.

Darlene's parents are completely at a loss as to how to help her and are currently in own marital counseling with a coworker at your agency. Darlene is fairly open and will talk with you about everything but the vacation incident.

That should give us enough information to formulate an idea about Darlene. After we present the theories, we can demonstrate that there is a different approach and focus to Darlene's presenting issues depends on the theory.

We divide the theoretical frameworks into categories that make them easier to understand. These categories are person-centered theories, behavioral theories, cognitive-behavioral theories, psychodynamic theories, and family systems theories. Table 8.1 outlines the major focus and primary features of these categories. We apply the theories to Darlene's case to show how application of a different theory might change the social work intervention with this client.

Table 8.1 Theories used to support social work intervention

	Person-Centered Theories
Theories	Existential theory
	Humanistic theory
	Empowerment
	Strengths perspective
General idea	Client and their environment determines their reality, active participants in the course of their own lives
	Determine behavior through the choices you make rather than nature or nurture
	Always in the process of developing
Theorists	Carl Rogers
	Kurt Goldstein
Human development	Core of each human is trustworthy and positive
	Create an environment of removing barriers to self-actualizing
	Regarded positively by others
Goals	Determined by the client
	Open to new experiences; develop good relationships
	Assume personal and social responsibilities
Helper's role	Be there
	Ability to develop and maintain relationship
	Unconditional positive regard
	Must be in psychological contact with one another
	Must help client experience anxiety for incongruence to motivate change
	Must be yourself
	Accept and appreciate the client as she or he is
	Empathetic; your values remain at the door
	Empathy and unconditional regard must be felt by the client
Assessment	Person-centered perspective
	Client's assessment more critical than yours
Techniques and process	Experience of being cared for and sense of freedom to express anything
	Slow unfolding of one's attitudes and perceptions
	Gradual movement toward less defensiveness about feelings
	Awareness of incongruities and factors
	A more accurate perception of self, problems, and relationships
	Increase in strength
	Gradual but definite sense of integrations of ideal and real self

	Behavioral Theories
Theories	Behavior modification
General idea	Principle of learning and conditioning (shows how behavior is developed, acquired, changed, and eliminated)
	Focus on internal, covert behaviors involved in learning
	Nature verses nurture
	Tabula Rasa (Latin for "blank slate")
Theorists	John B. Watson
	B. F. Skinner
	Ivan Petrovich Pavlov
	Mary Cover Jones
Human development	Behaviors and measures
	Conditioning/response/stimulus
	Extinction/reinforcement
	Shaping vicarious learning
	Socialization
Goals	Assist clients in acquiring new behavior, modifying behaviors, or eliminating undesirable or maladaptive behaviors
Helper's role	Instructor
	Reconditioner
	Coach
	Consultant
	Researcher
	Paraphrase and ask questions
Assessment	Behavioral interview
	Understand clients' behavior problems
	Antecedents and consequences
	Rating scales observations
Techniques and process	Positive and negative consequences
	Actively collaborate
	Instructive model
	Contingency management
	Desensitization
	Counterconditioning, modeling, and assertiveness training

Cognitive-Behavioral Theories	
Theories	Rational-emotive behavior therapy
	Cognitive therapy
	Cognitive-behavioral therapy
	Task-centered theory
General idea	Looking at thought and how it changes behavior
	Clients' difficulties are result of problems with cognitive process
	Time limited
	Educational approach
Theorists	Albert Ellis
	Aaron Beck
	Donald Meichenbaum
Human development	Human information process
	Active participants in creating their own reality through perceptions and prescribed experience/meaning
	How information is processed in behavior and feeling, which then creates behavior and personality problems
	Cognitive distortions
Goals	Assist client in identifying, challenging, and changing cognitions that negatively affect feelings and behaviors
	Work on self-interest, social interest, tolerance, flexibility, acceptance, commitment, risk taking, higher tolerance of frustration and taking responsibility for thoughts and feelings and actions
Helper's role	Consultant, trainer, educator, or collaborator
	Differs depending on the theory
Assessment	Assess the thought preceding, during, and following behavior
	Identify dysfunctional thoughts
Techniques and process	Cognitive restructuring

Psychodynamic Theories	
Theories	Drive theories
	Ego psychology
	Interpersonal theories
	Object relations theory
General idea	Nature verses nurture
	Mental activity combined with strength
	View people as energy, health is availability of energy and problems are static energy, release of energy
Theorists	Sigmund Freud
	Erik Erikson
	Anna Freud
Human development	Stages of development
	Defense mechanisms
	Id, ego, and superego
	Psychosocial involvement in the environment
	Emphasis on relationship and how to relate to others
	Relationships develop
Goals	Create significant change in personality structure and behavior
	Increase awareness of drives
	Strengthen ego and its defenses
Helper's role	Present clients with situation or relationship
	Project feelings, needs, past conflicts, templates, and other issues
Assessment	Indirectly or by inference, behaviorally oriented helper, projective techniques (tests)
Techniques and process	Transference neurosis
	Regress to improve
	Mirroring or idealizing
	Disconnection of self from relationships

Family Systems Theories	
Theories	Communication
	Structural
	Intergenerational
	Strategic and solution focused
	Systems theory
	Attachment
General idea	Consistent arrangement of things related or connected to form unity or to operate as a whole
	Approach equilibrium
	Cannot understand individuals without assessing system in which they are embedded
	Families in context of neighborhood, community, and social system
	Whole system change
	Focus on interpersonal relationships
Theorists	Virginia Satir
	Salvator Minuchin
	Murray Bowen
	Jay Haley
Human development	Subsytems boundaries
	Alignments, disengagement, enmeshment
	Differentiation, triangulation
	Focus on solutions
Goals	Support and enhance the system so as to better serve the individuals
	Change the system
Helper's role	Catalysts for change in families
	Emphasize communication patterns, and teach new communication, practice/rehearse
	Who the helper is is critical, as is the relationship he or she develops
Assessment	Observe communication, structure, interactions in a family to assess nature of problem
	Ecomaps and genograms
Techniques and process	Family sculpting
	Family roles
	Changing reclaiming roles
	Manipulations of the system
	Paradoxical interventions
	Ecomaps and genograms

Thoughts to ponder

Look over table 8.1.

Do you need more in-depth information?

Is there a category of theories that you already feel comfortable with?

Is there a category of theories that is hard for you to work with because you don't believe the premise or think it is too complicated?

Application of Theory to a Case

The usual process of working with a client, after taking a full biopsychosocial assessment (including genogram and ecomap), would be to get a good understanding of what the client's goals are for treatment, thus defining what will occur in the social work sessions you will be having with her. Once you know the goals, there are two tasks to complete. The first is to choose a theory, and the second is to form a treatment plan. In choosing a theoretical framework, you need to think about what the client wants to accomplish, how much time you have to accomplish the goal, and how comfortable you are with the theory.

Notice the order of those tasks. Often, because of the limited time we are allowed to be with clients, we are rushed to develop a treatment plan. So we may not spend enough time helping clients articulate what they are hoping to accomplish. This step is critical because it is the foundation of the treatment you will provide. If in the process other goals are accomplished, that is good. However, you need to honor the client's ideas as well as any ideas that you may come up with on your own.

The amount of time that is allotted for treatment is determined in a variety of ways. Sometimes it is determined by the client's insurance, and sometimes by the agency or program policy. Agencies determine the time allowed for client intervention either by the way the program was originally designed, or because the agency has received grant money that dictates the length of client treatment. Finally, your level of comfort with the theory depends on how well you paid attention in classes that discussed theory, and how much practice you have had with a specific theory.

Once you have chosen a theory, you can develop your treatment plan. We will discuss the formulation of a treatment plan in the subsequent chapter. At this point we will look at each category of theories presented in table 8.1. We will help you decide what theory to use based on the client's needs and how long you have to work.

Application of Humanistic Theories. By choosing to use the humanistic theories, you are looking at Darlene as an individual. What does she want? How does she perceive the problem? What choices has she made in her life that have gotten her to this point? What does she bring to the treatment that will assist her in the treatment process? What areas that she wants to change will she need support in? In order to answer these questions, you will want to develop a strong relationship with the client. The theory has you focus on the process and the relationship, not the problem specifically. During the initial assessment, while you are getting information, you will be exploring and developing the relationship between you and Darlene.

When probing for the answers to these questions, Darlene may tell you she likes to take chances and risks. Breaking the rules to her is fun, and she usually gets away with it. She may tell you that the only problem she sees is that she got caught and that she really doesn't want to change, except to be more careful the next time. You know by the way she talks about her escapades not only that she is serious about continuing her behavior, but that she is very smart (since she has been shoplifting for years and has been caught only once). Her goals for treatment would be to make everyone happy so they would get off her back and she can resume her normal activities.

You can certainly work with Darlene on talking about how to develop trust, and how to stay out of trouble so she no longer has a probation officer. But you have other options as well. Using her intelligence as a strength, walk her through her life options, college, jobs, legal records, probation, jail, and parole and see what her plans are for the future. Has she thought far ahead? Does she think her behavior now will interfere with her plans? Is she developmentally mature enough to have the foresight to see how today's behavior will affect her behavior later on? This may seem like a lot of questions to ask, but it helps you and Darlene agree to treatment issues and helps you see what strengths you have to work with while she is in treatment. The focus stays on Darlene. You ask the questions, and the quality of the relationship you have developed with her will allow her to answer in a way that helps her address her goals of getting out of trouble. She may also be helped to gain insight as to what motivates her to be in trouble and how to avoid trouble, in the future.

Obviously, because of our space constraints, this is an abbreviated version of the treatment process. But the general idea of humanistic theories is to start where the client is, develop a relationship with him or her, and help the client go where he or she wants to be, hopefully adding other pieces to the treatment to enrich it all the more.

Application of Behavior Theories. When using behavior theories, your role as the social worker is to help extinguish the behavior that is not wanted. This means you need to focus on the issues before you, not so much on the relationship. You would work with Darlene on how to get rid of the unacceptable or inappropriate behavior. You would want to understand what happens before and after the shoplifting that prompts or perpetuates the shoplifting. Your assessment will focus on the motivation behind the shoplifting, the benefits, risks, and consequences. Maybe the good outweighs the bad for shoplifting. Your role then would be to increase the negative consequences so that Darlene would want to stop, or to increase the positives so that she is willing to stop. In this case, shoplifting is an unacceptable behavior because it is against the law. You could develop a system of punishments when the behavior occurs, or you could offer rewards if it does not occur.

Application of Cognitive-Behavioral Theories. Cognitive-behavioral theories differ from behavioral theories in that you want to change the client's thought process, which will then change the behavior. In behavioral theories, you just want to extinguish the behaviors; the thought process is not considered. So when using cognitive-behavioral therapy with Darlene, you would want to understand how she thinks and talks about her behavioral difficulties. Listen carefully to her word choices when she discusses shoplifting. Is it an adventure, is it rewarding, and is it viewed as acceptable behavior to her ("everyone does it")? If so, your goal would be to help change her viewpoint about shoplifting. Restructuring her thoughts, by example, stories, and changing her word choices, will help her see that this is unacceptable behavior that she needs to change. Once the thoughts change, the behavior disappears.

Application of Psychodynamic Theories. Psychodynamic theories look at the unresolved issues of the past that create the current problems. They ask why a problem exists; solve the "why," and the problem will stop. Of all the theories, these take the longest because they involve exploration of the past. Does Darlene steal because she feels unwanted because she is adopted? Does she steal because she has a bad reputation and feels that she has to live up to the reputation? Is she "stuck" in a stage of development? If so, which one and why? Although this theory takes longer, it usually has a longer-lasting effect on the client, because the past issues are resolved and therefore shouldn't cause any other difficulty for the client in the future.

Application of Family Systems Theories. To use family systems theories in the case of Darlene, the social worker would involve the entire family. He or she would explore with the parent whether their relationship problems have any bearing on the problems that Darlene is having. He or she would explore how the issues about consistent rule breaking have been dealt with in the family. The social worker would also want to know about other stressors and the current status of all the relationships in the family now. Who talks to whom? Who does Darlene get along with better—Mom or Dad? All of this assessment material would help them figure out what might be altered in their family that would change Darlene's behavior. The assumption here is that if you live within families, they impact you in some way. How are the family relationships manifesting themselves in Darlene's behavior? Once the relationships are changed, "put in homeostasis" or balance, Darlene will act appropriately again.

As you can see by each of the short explanations of the theories, the result is the same. They all address Darlene's behavior of shoplifting. Each theory took a different approach but got the same basic outcome. If it were possible for Darlene to go through each theory, and not remember the other, she would express different secondary benefits, such as, she thinks about consequences more (behavioral theory), she is more concerned about how she affects her family and how they affect her (family systems theory), but in each case the shoplifting behavior is gone.

At the beginning of the chapter, we noted that some social workers would use an eclectic viewpoint. They would try a little of everything. They would get the family involved, explore how Darlene feels about her adoption, and look at the relationships with her parents. They might also try offering rewards and punishments and increasing Darlene's strengths so that she doesn't succumb to peer pressure. Sometimes it makes more sense to come at a case from different viewpoints to extract the problem from the person, but it does not always work as well. It is not the purest use of theory, and it is important for you to know what the theory says as well as what works.

When talking to your supervisor about theory, ask about what he or she thinks works best with the client population you have at the agency where you are doing your field placement. Discuss your supervisor's favorite theories and see if you can formulate an idea about what you particularly like about each theory and what you dislike. This discussion may help you decide where you need to focus your time in theory development. After all, you want to choose a theory that is effective for the clients you are currently treating.

Integration of other course material	
HBSE	What theories of development would be useful for you to know about in your field placement?
Policy	How does policy dictate what theory is used in your social work practice?
Practice	Do you feel comfortable with any particular theory now that could guide your practice in social work? What else do you need to know about the theory to use it effectively? What if you are a macro social worker? Could you use these theories? Why or why not? Are there macropractice theories that you need to know?
Research	What theory would you choose to use for a study on the improvement of one of your clients over time?

Resources

Cognitive-Behavioral Therapy
http://www.cognitivetherapy.com/

Cambridge Center for Behavioral Studies
http://www.behavior.org/

Freudian, Lacanian, and Object Relations Theory
http://homepage.newschool.edu/~quigleyt/vcs/psychoanalysis.html

Allyn and Bacon Family Therapy Web site
http://www.abacon.com/famtherapy/index.html

Attachment Theory
http://www.personalityresearch.org/attachment.html

Personality Theories
http://www.ship.edu/~cgboeree/rogers.html

Task-Centered Social Work Practice and the Family
http://www.geocities.com/taskcentered/index.html

Have you come across a social work book you want to read in the future? Make your book list here.

Title	Author	Year	Publisher

Chapter 9
Treatment Planning

The further we go into the semester, the more contact you should be having with clients. Whether you are running more group, or are involved in case management, individual sessions, or community meetings, you can expect that your contact has purpose. That purpose is to assist with one of the goals the client established when entering treatment at your agency. To be sure that every contact you have with the client is as profitable as possible, it is important that you be aware of the treatment goals. The treatment plans are in the client file. Every agency has a different format for the treatment plan, but they essentially all want to know the same information. This chapter will let you know what a treatment plan includes, how to determine what the plan should be, and how to word the goals and objectives. We will continue to use Darlene's case, presented in chapter 8.

Developing a Treatment Plan

After completing the biopsychosocial, genogram, and ecomap, it is time to figure out what the client is hoping to accomplish by coming to your agency. Often clients have a vague idea of what they are hoping to achieve but don't know how to get there. Often they are open to other suggestions that you can make, based on what you heard them say in their biopsychosocial. A good way to go about setting up the treatment plan is to start with the client. Ask the client what it is that he or she wants to work on. If you see some obvious thing that you think the client may want to work on, you can ask if that is also of interest. The conversation about things that you want to suggest should be at the end of your session, after the client has told you what he or she wants to work on. At that time, you would schedule the next session with your client.

Take the information you received in the initial assessment (biopsychosocial), and talk to your supervisor. Talk about the important incidents in the client's life and the goals the client wishes to achieve. Give your supervisor your impressions of the client and what goals you thought you would add to the goals the client identified to work toward in treatment. Your supervisor may have suggestions for you based on the information you have gathered and presented.

Choose a theory to use, based upon the client's thoughts and desires, your time frame, and the agency treatment philosophy, if there is one. Once you have selected a theory, you can establish the formal treatment goals and objectives. When the goals for treatment are established, you will need to present them again to your client for approval, clearly indicating what the goals are that he or she wanted to work on, and how to plan to accomplish those goals (the objectives). The form in

Darlene's treatment plan (table 9.1) can be used to develop a treatment plan if your agency does not have a form. Most treatment plans will have the same information in them as the form used here, but it may have a different order or leave out one or two components. For example, we have seen treatment plans that list the strengths but leave out the obstacles and vice versa.

When working on a treatment plan, remember the client is the expert on his or her life. You do not live in the client's shoes twenty-four hours a day, seven days a week. It is your job to help him or her figure out how to avoid and clear the obstacles, but it is the client's responsibility to explain what it is he or she is willing to do and what is realistic to achieve. The clients' right to self-determination is important here. Clients have the right to choose what they will do. Remember the NASW Code of Ethics section on self-determination (section 1.02).

> Social workers respect and promote the right of clients to self-determination and assist clients in their efforts to identify and clarify their goals. Social workers may limit clients' right to self-determination when, in the social workers' professional judgment, clients' actions or potential actions pose a serious, foreseeable, and imminent risk to themselves or others.

Most times you and your client will be in agreement, but when you think something should be done that the client doesn't want to do, it can be very frustrating and you should be prepared for that. For instance, you may think that Darlene should complete her homework to improve her status in school. She may say that is not important to her, and she is not willing to do her homework or improve her status in school. Your best bet is to really look for the things that will motivate your client to complete treatment. Sometimes this motivation is a reward for finishing, like completing legal obligations. Other times it is just feeling better because the problem is solved.

What you offer any client is the ability to hear what the problem is and offer suggestions on how to solve the problem. The goal becomes the solution to the problem, and the suggestions on how to solve the problem are the objectives. The easier the objectives the more likely the client is to complete them and stay motivated. Be sure that the client knows what you are doing every step of the way. But before you can write the goals and objectives, you need to have a good understanding of the theory that you are going to use, because it will make a difference in the treatment plan. After explaining goals and objectives, we will develop two treatment plans for Darlene, using two different theories from the categories outlined in chapter 8.

Differences between Goals and Objectives

A goal is a very broad and general statement of what the client wants to accomplish, such as "elimination of illegal activities." The objective is usually phrased as a statement, "to eliminate" or to "increase" something that is difficult for your client. The goal is usually not measurable, which means that it is vague, and the objectives are the specifics.

Goals usually fall into four categories: health (mental, physical, emotional), legal affairs, education/vocation, and relationships (family, friends, significant others). After completing the biopsychosocial you should sort out the goals into those four categories. Prioritize goals based on what the client wants to work on first. If there is an emergency in a particular area, you need to deal with that first (e.g., a medical condition that has to be addressed, like the client has just been diagnosed with cancer and needs to start treatment immediately). If there is no emergency, some of the goals could be worked on at the same time, although some may take longer to complete. For example, someone may need to work on self-esteem, relationships with others, and getting a college degree. All these goals can be worked on at the same time, but the college degree may take longer if the client isn't in school already.

Sometimes goals are clearly evident. If the client has legal or medical problems, you want to get those addressed as quickly as possible. Other treatment goals are not as readily apparent. Examples are improving relationships with friends or decreasing cursing and swearing because the client thinks that is an increasing problem.

Objectives are the step-by-step actions that will be taken to achieve the goals. In the case of getting a college degree, if you are working with a high school student, objectives include successfully completing high school, taking the SAT or ACT exams, choosing which colleges to visit, visiting colleges, writing applications, making a final decision on which university, attending the school, choosing a major, registering, and successfully completing all courses. You may be thinking that it isn't really a social worker's job to help someone decide what college to go to. However, some people need support and supervision for many of these steps. Helping to make the decision about a school, or really focusing on completing high school, may be something the social worker would help with. Seeing the consequences of their decisions and understanding how to make a decision are skills that lots of people do not have. A social worker can help a client with these skills.

Objectives are concrete changes desired by clients. Objectives are readily measurable and observable because they are detailed and very specific. Objectives are also smaller steps to reach goals. List every step needed to achieve the goals and make sure it is reasonable and attainable. For instance, if someone is having financial difficulty, you would not list winning this week's state lottery as an objective, because it is not attainable and realistic. Objectives need to be time limited, which means that steps get completed in a reasonable time period that will not ruin the client's motivation or discourage him or her because it is so far away. Look at a high school student's goal of getting a college degree. That is at least a five-year goal (senior year and four years at college), which can seem insurmountable, especially when you're in the middle of writing papers and studying for exams!

When we say that objectives are measurable and observable, we are talking about being able to see changes or to measure them through a change in reported behavior by the client or those that see him or her frequently. Once you have all the objectives written, you need to determine four things:

> How will you measure the change?

> How will you prioritize the objectives (which ones need to be completed first)?

> Who will complete the tasks?

> When will the objectives be completed?

Finally, to complete a treatment plan like the one for Darlene, you need to think about what strengths the client has to successfully accomplish the goals. These strengths include systemwide strengths like family and friends as well as personal characteristics that the client may have. After listing the strengths that will assist the client, list the obstacles for the client. What in the client's system will impede his or her ability to attain the goal? Is there any way you can help activate the strengths and eliminate the obstacles?

Operationalizing a Treatment Plan with a Theory

Table 9.1 shows you how the treatment differs for Darlene depending on the theory that we use. For this exercise, we use a cognitive-behavioral approach and a family systems approach to see the treatment differences.

Table 9.1 Treatment plans based on two theories

Cognitive-Behavioral Approach

Problem	Goal	Objectives	Responsibility	Time frame	Evaluation procedure
Darlene is in trouble with the law.	To stop Darlene's illegal activity	1. Have Darlene research the legal consequences of using alcohol and drugs and of shoplifting. a. Allow Darlene access to online information and the library to find legal repercussions. b. Have Darlene meet with local police juvenile officer to hear stories of other adolescents who have had difficulty with the law.	Darlene	2 weeks	Written report to social worker
		2. Have Darlene attend an Outward Bound program that teaches "natural highs" and communication skills. a. Provide structured risk-taking behaviors for 1 week. b. Increase her ability to express thoughts to parents.	Outward Bound program and Darlene	1 month	Certificate of completion

Table 9.1 Continued Treatment plans based on two theories

Problem	Goal	Objectives	Responsibility	Time frame	Evaluation procedure
	Anticipated Obstacles ■ Darlene's willingness to meet with officer ■ Parents' willingness to follow through with Outward Bound program				
	Anticipated Strengths ■ Darlene's need for challenge and excitement				
Darlene is having difficulty in school.	To improve Darlene's progress in school	1. Have Darlene tested for learning disabilities. 2. Discuss with Darlene her thoughts about education and any importance it may have to her. 3. Find out what Darlene's goals for the future are and develop plan to achieve.	Child study team Social worker and Darlene Social worker, guidance counselor, and parents	3 months 2 weeks 1 month	Written report of assessment Self-report Self-report
	Anticipated Obstacles ■ Darlene's lack of focus on academics ■ Finding a tutor who will try creative approaches to learning				

Table 9.1 Continued Treatment plans based on two theories

Problem	Goal	Objectives	Responsibility	Time frame	Evaluation procedure
	Anticipated Strengths ■ Darlene enjoying one-on-one attention from tutor ■ Finding ways to access her career choices				
Family System-Approach					
Darlene is in trouble with the law.	To stop Darlene's illegal activity	Provide supervision to Darlene on all out-of-house trips.	Parents	3 months	Self-report from parents
	To build relationship with parents to rebuild trust	1. Darlene to spend quality time with each parent individually one evening a week.	Parents and Darlene	2 months	Self-report from Darlene
		2. Darlene and parents to increase number of meals together. a. Choose meals to eat together. b. Choose topics of discussion.	Parents and Darlene	3 months	Self-report from parents
	Anticipated Obstacles ■ Parents' work schedules ■ Parents' consistency and willingness				

Table 9.1 Continued Treatment plans based on two theories

Problem	Goal	Objectives	Responsibility	Time frame	Evaluation procedure
	Anticipated Strengths ■ Instilling rituals into family lifestyle ■ Desire of parents to be closer to daughter				
Darlene is having difficulty in school.	To improve Darlene's school progress	1. Have Darlene receive an hour of tutoring a week from her parents. 2. Establish clear-cut expectations about grades in classes. 3. Devise study schedule, routine, and rules for homework time.	Family Family with teachers Family with social worker	Immediately Within 3 weeks Immediately	Self-report Self-report Written rules
	Anticipated Obstacles ■ Darlene's unwillingness ■ Parents' time and understanding of homework *Anticipated Strengths* ■ Communication with the school ■ Support emphasis for importance of school				

Notice the difference in the goals, objectives, and even more specifically, the people responsible for the objectives. The cognitive-behavioral goals are more about interaction and clearly understanding and then changing the thought process. The family systems approach is more about the collaborative effort of the Darlene's system to see that things change. Every problem will follow the same guidelines after you select which theoretical framework to work with. Neither set of treatment objectives is better than the other, at face value. After learning who your client is (better than in the brief summary you have of Darlene), you will be able to choose the best theoretical framework.

Sometimes people intermix theories because each set of objectives listed here has good ideas and could have a synergistic effect if they were all used, thereby increasing the chance of success with Darlene.

Spend a moment thinking about a client at your internship. Use the blank treatment plan at the end of the chapter to write a brief treatment for that client. Remember to select a theory first.

Thoughts to ponder

Did you have difficulty writing the treatment plan?

What areas were most problematic for you?

Did you make the treatment plan reasonable?

Were you able to see the distinctions between the plans based on the two theories?

What are your concerns about developing a treatment plan?

How close does your agency come to creating treatment plans as explained here?

What are your thoughts about the treatment-plan process at your agency?

Integration of other course material

HBSE	Which part of your assessment will help you with your treatment plan?
Policy	What are the time frames needed for developing a treatment plan in your agency from the time that the client enters your program? Who dictates that policy?
Practice	What are the appropriate ways to develop this treatment plan?
Research	How does this treatment plan expedite your research for this particular case?

Resources

Wodarski, J. S., Rapp-Paglicci, L. A., Dulmus, C. N., & Jongsma, A. E. (2000). *The social work and human services treatment planner*. New York: Wiley.

United Methodist Family Services
http://www.empowerkids.org/images/treatmentplans.pdf

University of Westminster, London Alternative Care
http://www.wmin.ac.uk/sih/page-590-smhp=435

**Do you have these?
Write about this aspect of yourself.**

Problem	Goal	Objectives	Responsibility	Time frame	Evaluation procedure
	Anticipated Obstacles				
	Anticipated Strength				
	Anticipated Obstacles				
	Anticipated Strength				

Chapter 10
Teamwork: Your Supervisor and You

At this point in your field experience, we expect that you are now clear about your role within the agency and that you have a number of responsibilities in the agency. These responsibilities may include case management, group facilitation, linking clients to resources, and other functions of a social worker. You should also be getting ongoing supervision with your field supervisor. Each social work program has a standard requirement for supervision for students in the field. This standard is usually an hour per week with a qualified supervisor, preferably an MSW.

Supervisors' Function

Supervision cements the cornerstone of your relationship with your supervisor. You began this relationship at the interview where you received a good understanding of the mission of the agency and about what you would do while an intern. This chapter focuses on what that relationship entails and how it is significant to you. What follows are some general tips that may help you understand how to use your supervisor for supervision and what to expect from that process.

One of the things you have probably figured out by now is that social work agencies are very busy and there is never a dull moment. This means that your supervisor is busy as well. Rarely in today's world do supervisors have a single role in the agency. They may carry a caseload, write grants, serve on several committees, and maintain a relationship with other agencies. Supervisors generally agree to take a student intern for a few reasons. First, someone was willing to supervise them when they were an intern, and taking an intern is a way to give back to the profession or to a specific social work program (maybe the one they graduated from). Second, supervisors see supervision as a way of providing more services to their clients in a financially responsible and clinically appropriate way. Third, supervisors like to keep their skills fresh, and having an intern keeps them abreast of the current professional landscape in social work. Finally, they may enjoy training new social workers and helping them develop into professionals. In rare instances, the supervisor's supervisor has agreed to take an intern and has not told your supervisor about you until right before or at your arrival. Regardless of why you are there, supervisors are very busy people, yet are responsible for providing you with a good experience and exposure to the realities of social work.

For most of you, this is probably not your first job, but it might be your first professional job. If you have worked outside of the social work field, you had a supervisor; in a broad sense, every boss you ever had was a supervisor. However, a manager at a restaurant or fast-food chain is not as concerned about developing your professional skills and your personal development. Your field supervisor is concerned with both. Your supervisor at the agency is concerned about the well-being and safety of the clients. To address that dual role, supervision entails three components: administrative, educational, and supportive.

Administrative supervision deals with enforcing agency policy and scheduling work load and everyone's working hours. Your supervisor will be give you an understanding of agency policy, work duties, your schedule, and how you will be evaluated. Administrative supervision takes a great deal of time, since supervisors have to administer the work of the unit they are responsible for. They not only schedule work hours, enforce agency policy, and distribute cases, but also know about what every worker under their supervision is doing, including what they are doing with each client case. You will come to understand the importance of team meetings as well as individual supervision as you watch your supervisor engage in administrative supervision.

The second role of a supervisor is educational supervision. In this role, the supervisor reinforces what you have learned in the classroom, enhancing and elaborating information as needed for that particular agency, and discusses cases with you. The supervisor will explore your theoretical framework and how you are applying it to your cases. As your supervisor is providing educational supervision, you will finally connect all that you have been learning directly to your work with clients. The supervisor also looks at the educational needs of the entire staff and works to ensure that they receive the educational experiences that they need or want. This could take the form of scheduling in-service training at the agency, sending staff to continuing-education workshops, developing a resource library at the agency for anyone to use, and even developing policy that reimburses employees for tuition spent on furthering their education.

The third role is supportive supervision. It means offering understanding when you have a difficult case, or suggesting how to proceed. Supportive supervision is given every time your supervisor helps you understand your feelings about how the internship is going. Supportive supervision occurs on a regular basis at the agency when employees need to change their work schedule because of a personal problem, or when they need time off to deal with a death in the family, or when they need to seek outside counseling for a drug or alcohol problem. Supportive supervision is not therapy—its focus is to enable the employee (or intern) to cope effectively with their work.

Very often you will be able to analyze a supervision session after the fact, to fully understand which type of supervision your supervisor has given you.

Details of Supervision

How should supervision be formatted and scheduled? Supervision can be ongoing before and after your task (talking to a client, facilitating a meeting, establishing a discharge plan, etc.), can be a preestablished hour set aside each week, or can be group supervision with other social workers or interns that your supervisor is responsible for.

The NASW Code of Ethics offers some clear guidance on the issue of supervision and consultation, in section 3.01.

> (a) Social workers who provide supervision or consultation should have the necessary knowledge and skill to supervise or consult appropriately and should do so only within their areas of knowledge and competence.

> (b) Social workers who provide supervision or consultation are responsible for setting clear, appropriate, and culturally sensitive boundaries.

> (c) Social workers should not engage in any dual or multiple relationships with supervisees in which there is a risk of exploitation of or potential harm to the supervisee.

> (d) Social workers who provide supervision should evaluate supervisees' performance in a manner that is fair and respectful.

Generally speaking, once you are an MSW for a few years you will probably be asked to be a supervisor. Frequently, supervision in social work is an elective course when (if) you get your MSW. Think about taking that course if the idea of being a supervisor appeals to you. If you don't take an elective on supervision, you can probably pick up a course on supervision post-MSW while getting your continuing-education units (CEUs).

How to Prepare for Supervision

Our first suggestion for how to prepare for your supervision session is to think ahead and develop an agenda for your supervisor. At the end of this chapter is a sample form that you can use to develop your agenda. If you have a particular question, write it down or bring the material with you. If you are going to discuss a client's case, have the entire file with you, organized so that you can readily find the information you need. That may mean writing some notes and questions, so that you can find what you need during your allotted supervision time.

As an aside, we realize that you may not know exactly how to prepare for a meeting. Always come to any meeting with a pen, your calendar, and a pad of paper. You can assume that at the meeting you will always set another meeting date and time, and that you will always have action items to take care of after the meeting, which is why you bring your calendar and a note pad. You should know the topic for the meeting and be prepared to share information that you have on the subject. It is a good idea to write down any questions that you have about the topic. If you need to travel for the meeting, be sure to leave enough time to get there and not be late. You want to be on time for the meeting, whether everyone else is on time or not. Being on time includes getting something to drink, going to the restroom, and being in your seat and ready no later than the start of the meeting. These helpful hints should help you look quite professional and very mature at your internship!

Sometimes your supervisor will not know the answer to your questions. That is OK. Although he or she is a more experienced social worker than you, your supervisor is still human and not perfect! He or she may need to consult someone, or may refer you to another source to get the information. Both ways will help you get the information and teach you at the same time, so it matters not which approach is used.

Make sure that you are clear both in asking your questions and in what you hear when listening to the answers. Your questions and the answers will impact how you service your clients, and everyone wants to be sure that client care is safe and accurate. You need to remember the answers to all of your questions for your supervisor. That is how you will build your knowledge of the field and the services your agency offers. Most likely similar issues will continue to come up throughout your internship. Show your competence and intelligence to your clients and your supervisors by not having to ask the same questions over and over.

Check the contract that you and your supervisor negotiated. When you developed the contract, it should have been inclusive enough to expose you to every aspect of social work your agency provides, especially the components on your evaluation for your specific program. If you have a second semester of internship in your, school you might want to renegotiate the learning contract based upon your knowledge of the agency and your skills as they have developed by midyear.

Your internship is an extension of the classroom, and your supervisor is there to guide you through the "real" social work cases. You can think of your supervisor as another one of your professors—guiding you and helping you grow, both personally and professionally.

Negotiating What You Need

What happens when your supervision does not go as planned? In spite of all the effort you make to develop and maintain a good relationship with your supervisor, things go wrong. Sometimes the easy flowing dialogue/teaching described above does not work out exactly as planned. It could be your supervisor is overcommitted and doesn't have enough time, it could be lack of work and you are bored, it could be a personality clash that is hard to cope with, or it could be your skills and work ethic are not what the agency expected and are causing difficulty. It could also be a myriad of other reasons. You and your supervisor will need to work out these difficulties.

As two people in the same profession striving for the same goal, which is the care and treatment of your clients, you need some confluence of ideas and a comfortable working relationship. Any difficulty you are experiencing has to be addressed. Yet you are concerned about bringing up the issue because this person, your supervisor, is responsible for your evaluation and you would like a good grade for class. You might also wonder if you are right about certain things, and you don't want to confront your supervisor—after all he or she has more experience than you and has worked at the agency longer. Who are you to be second-guessing or guiding your supervisor and the process? This is a perfect time for you to understand that you need to address uncomfortable issues. Concerns should be remedied as they come up. That way the concerns don't fester and result in a mess. We encourage all students to try to address problems with their supervisors. If they are unsuccessful, we as faculty will intervene. We don't get involved right away, so that students can develop the ability to advocate for themselves and clients.

Chances are, though, that you don't like confrontation and get very anxious about having to approach your supervisor about anything remotely challenging or questioning. Besides, you may even get uncomfortable about fighting with family or friends. However, what we are talking about doesn't have to end up in a fight and isn't exactly confrontation. It is being assertive and standing up for your rights. Or it is advocacy and standing up for the rights of your clients. Either way, advocacy or asserting yourself are essential skills you will need in both your personal and professional life, so it is worth spending time learning how to discuss uncomfortable issues with your supervisor.

Thoughts to ponder

How do you let your supervisor know that you don't understand or that you feel as though you lack knowledge and/or experience to do what he or she has asked?

Which type of supervision (supportive, educational, or administrative) does your supervisor use most often with you? Is that what you need?

Assertiveness

Being assertive, whether you are advocating for yourself or for a client, is really about being able to communicate what you are trying to say without violating the rights of others, humiliating them, or being aggressive. Aggressiveness comes when you are selfish and destructive to others, maybe being demanding or inconsiderate in the process. If you are not assertive or aggressive, you are usually passive, which comes across to others as weak, self-sacrificing, and compliant. When we look at these traits, it is sometimes easier to view them as a continuum, with assertiveness in the middle and the ultimate professional goal.

Passive	Assertive	Aggressive

It is not easy to be assertive. Finding the right balance of saying what needs to be said without going overboard into aggressiveness, especially in a new situation and with a supervisor, is very important. It is a skill that social workers need to master so they can successfully advocate for their clients and themselves.

So how do you have an assertive conversation? Great question, and the fast answer is practice. If you are traditionally not someone who lets people know what you want or need, this will be very important for you. The steps are simple but take practice. As you practice, it will get easier. Sometimes you may sound too aggressive, sometimes you may feel that things didn't go well or got worse; when that occurs, you have ended up closer to being passive on the continuum. There are four basic steps to being assertive.

1. Be clear and specific about what you are looking for. Start with "I" statements and own what you are saying. "I want," "I need," "I feel," and "I think" are all great ways to start your conversation. Continue being clear and state details about what you want and why.

2. Always be direct, open, and honest. Although it is easy to talk to people who aren't involved in a particular issue, you will avoid gossip and office politics if you direct your comments to the person you have concerns about and only that person. Sometimes we catch ourselves talking to others, "because you were wondering if this was just a problem for you or if others were experiencing this." But if you talk about others, especially your supervisor, don't expect to be respected or considered professional.

3. Own your message all the way through; continue with "I" statements. Don't bring anyone else into the discussion unless you have been appointed spokesperson for a particular group of people and have been clear from the beginning that you speak for them all. (Right: I feel I have too many cases to handle. Wrong: I feel I have too many cases and everybody else thinks so too.)

4. Ask for feedback about how you sounded and communicated. Be sure to carry out the dialogue about the issue first. Sometimes, depending on how the encounter goes, you may ask for feedback at a later time.

If you think you will be really anxious about being an advocate or being assertive, write down key points and keep the rules with you during the discussion. Try really hard to stay on topic and cover everything. You don't want to revisit the topic again if you don't have to. If you successfully assert yourself, you should feel more confident, build respect with your supervisor, develop a sense of control, and learn how to compromise without feeling as though you lost completely or are helpless.

Timing can be very important when you are discussing issues or trying to be assertive or advocate about an issue. Don't pop your head in the door five minutes before the end of the work day. If a crisis is occurring at work, that is probably a poor time as well. We suggest making an appointment and letting the person know this is an important topic to you. That way, you can hope to have his or her undivided attention.

Mastering the technique of being assertive will be beneficial for both your professional and personal life. A critical part of it is your nonverbal communication. If you say all the right things but accompany them with body language or facial expressions that are not congruent with your message, then you will defeat your purpose. Keep control of your voice tone, volume, and speed and your body motions. Ensure that the message received is assertive.

Classroom exercise

Pair off with a person in the class and role-play an instance where you wish that you could be more assertive. Preferably select an issue at your field placement, but if you don't have a field placement issue, a personal issue will also work. Play yourself and have your partner be your supervisor (or the person you have the issue with). Follow the four steps and practice the situation. Have your partner give you feedback about how he or she felt while you made your points, and then have him or her critique what you did and said. Then reverse the roles.

Shared Meaning

The result of your conversations should be shared meaning. You and your supervisor should be developing a mutual understanding and agreement. Gender and cultural issues are worth a mention here. Don't let culture or gender get in the way. Sometimes different cultures or the opposite sex communicates differently. Spend time making sure those differences do not cause a misunderstanding.

Professional Use of Self

Finally, use your supervisor to begin to develop your professional use of self. This term (more jargon) refers to learning about what it is about you (your personality, culture, gender, etc.) that you can use to your benefit as a social worker. Examples of this might include a sense of humor or your understanding of a specific religious issue because you are of that religion. Use your personal strengths, knowledge, and characteristics to develop your professional persona and style.

Supervisors can help you determine what these useful pieces of you are and how and when to incorporate them into your social work practice.

Thoughts to ponder

Perhaps professional use of self and assertiveness would be interesting topics for supervision this week!

Integration of other course material

HBSE   How did your supervisor assess your skills when you came to interview? What HBSE content did they use in making a decision about you?

Policy   What are the policies at your agency about how people become supervisors? Is specific training in supervision required?

Practice   How does developing a good supervisory relationship help your practice with clients? What does your practice class teach you about supervision?

Research   Are there any good research studies on the use of supervision in social work?

Resources

Assertiveness training
http://www.csusm.edu/caps/Assertiveness.html
http://www.psychologyinfo.com/treatment/assertiveness.html
http://mentalhelp.net/psyhelp/chap13/chap13e.htm

Kieran's Home Page, a tremendous site on supervision, from a social worker from New Zealand
http://www.geocities.com/kieranodsw/personal.htm

Supervision is a very important part of the field internship. Make sure you have a regular time for supervision every week with your field supervisor. Take time to make a brief agenda for each supervisory session, from asking questions to getting help on a particular case.

Date of supervision session _____

My agenda for supervision

Questions I have

Resources I think I need

Chapter 11
Finding Your Place in the Agency

No matter where you work—a school, hospital, nursing home, group home, or other agency—you are a part of a team. That team provides a comprehensive program of treatment for all the clients that enter into treatment with your agency. A comprehensive program needs a staff with an array of skill sets and talents. The staff comprises interdisciplinary teams of people who have a variety of degrees. Table 11.1 lists possible teams.

Table 11.1 Personnel in an interdisciplinary team

Type of service area	Possible treatment teams
Psychiatric hospital	Psychiatrist, RN, social worker, LPN, adjunctive therapist (recreational therapist, art therapist, etc.)
Nursing home	Medical doctor, nurse, social worker, dietician, physical therapist
School	Teacher, principal, social worker, learning disability consultant, school psychologist

Team Roles

The role of each person on the team will be based on the setting. In the psychiatric hospital, the psychiatrist generally heads the team, which is the typical medical model. Nurses may facilitate groups and are in charge of medicine and implementation of medical tests and vital signs. In the nursing home, a registered nurse is generally in charge of the team because the doctor is not always on site. The dietician will recommend proper diets in terms of quantity and the types of food that would be good for the individual based on his or her medical needs. In school settings, teachers lead the child study team. The psychologist and the learning consultant provide testing and observations necessary to complete and implement an individual education plan (IEP or treatment plan) for students who have learning disabilities. Social workers' roles vary based on the setting as well. Roles may include intake assessments, therapy sessions, and discharge (psychiatric hospitals); intake, family contact, and discharge planning (nursing home); and assessment and case management (schools).

As with all relationships, the treatment team needs to develop a rapport. The working relationships and the functioning of the team will define themselves based upon historic information (what has always been done), financial considerations (what the agency can afford), legal considerations (what the minimum personnel standards are for the team), and programmatic issues (what is needed for the current makeup of the team). All these factors will enter into the qualifications of the team members as well as how active a role they play. For instance, the nursing home may have a consulting psychiatrist. Not everyone in the nursing home needs a psychiatrist, however; so the psychiatrist will be used only as needed and is therefore not a regular member of the team. Another example may be a school district where the law requires schools to have access to a child study team. If the school district is small and is concerned about budgeting, however, those services may be contracted out to people who work for larger school districts or to new graduates who are less expensive than social workers and psychologists who have years of experience.

Once the team is formed, it must develop a working relationship with an understanding of what each person's responsibilities are. Again, responsibilities could be determined by job descriptions or legal constraints (e.g., social workers can't write prescriptions, so the doctor, physicians assistant, or nurse practioner must). The team must learn to communicate clearly with one another to be sure the client's needs are met in a timely manner that is economically feasible for the client and the agency and accurate in assessment, diagnosis, and treatment.

In order to communicate clearly, it is important that the team meet prior to seeing clients, to get to know one another. This is about knowing one another as *professionals*, not on a personal level. So questions about what type of degree you have, where you got it, how long and where you have been working, and what your experience is with the population you will be working with at this agency are all appropriate and critical to understanding the composition of the team. Other questions to consider are what you are really good at and what you dislike doing; then the team can use everyone's strengths for the benefits of the clients and offer support as needed for jobs that people dislike or cannot do as well.

While getting to know each other on the team, it would be a good time to negotiate tasks if they are not clearly defined or if they are flexible. Things like how often groups are held and who facilitates them can be up for negotiation. One of the benefits of working as a team is that you share the workload to minimize burnout and increase effectiveness.

Stages of Team Development

Anywhere from three to eight people can make up an interdisciplinary team. This is usually the same size as a therapeutic group. Teams will go through the typical stages of group development, and you should expect to be part of that development. Here we will describe the group stages of preaffiliation, power and control, intimacy, differentiation, and separation.

In the interdisciplinary team, preaffiliation involves feelings of ambivalence, fear, and anxiety. People generally don't take risks or disclose their feelings about their strengths and weaknesses or their concerns about the other members. If you were a social worker joining a preexisting team in a hospital, you would probably be professional but quiet and guarded about your contributions to the team or areas where you are unsure about your knowledge and skills.

The phase of power and control is where the negotiation of tasks comes up as well as the roles of each person. At this phase, you discuss who will have what responsibilities within the group. These responsibilities usually include contact with families and external agencies, arranging transportation, tests, ancillary equipment, report writing, chart documentation, discharge planning, therapy sessions and contact with the client. There certainly is enough to do. Perhaps some responsibilities have to rotate, while others belong specifically to one person and others are shared. All this is addressed in the power-and-control stage.

The third stage is intimacy. The fear and anxiety of preaffiliation stage is gone, roles and responsibilities were negotiated in the power-and-control stage, and you feel more comfortable about your role and the role of the team. The team comfortableness turns into a caring atmosphere about the general welfare of the other team members.

Intimacy then turns into stage four, which is differentiation. Team members have taught each other about their unique contribution to the team and have supported each other enough that team members can anticipate each other's next treatment action and understand fully their own contribution to the team.

In the final stage, separation, the group usually realizes that each member is an individual and is autonomous. An interdisciplinary treatment team does not separate for individuals to work autonomously. Rather, they come together as one efficient unit, working very well together for their clients.

Joining a Treatment Team

Treatment teams that work with very difficult clients or who stay together for a long time become very close. Usually this closeness transcends the professional relationship and develops into more personal relationships than we recommend for interns. Your relationship with any treatment team that you are placed with is temporary and tangential. In some cases, you may be perceived as an outsider and treated as such. In other cases, the team may welcome you with open arms, but recognize that you are an outsider and need to be incorporated into the team through the stages of the group process. How you are accepted will vary depending on what stage the team is in, the size of the team, and the personalities in it. Be cautious and professional about what you disclose about yourself and how you disclose it (we will discuss this further in the chapter on boundaries). As an intern, your job will be the same as the social worker who is your supervisor. If he or she is filing and developing treatment plans and finalizing discharge plans, you will be as well. If there is any area you want to learn or want to spend time observing, let your supervisor know. Treatment teams, especially those that have been together for a long time, work very fast and efficiently. You will need to show some initiative and let your supervisor know which part of the team responsibilities you want to handle. You may also need to ask what you are legally allowed to handle, because chances are that you cannot legally sign as the social worker on a treatment plan.

Treatment team meetings are usually held at varying times and days. If you can arrange your internship hours to be at the agency when the treatment team is meeting, do so. If you can't because of other commitments, try to arrange to be there at least once or twice during the semester. It is a worthwhile learning experience to observe a high-functioning interdisciplinary team in action. If you have class, talk to your teacher to see if you could have an excused absence.

We should also point out that not only do training and experience contribute to the unique personality of an interdisciplinary team, but culture, gender, and personality. Be aware of the number of people on your team. What are their genders? What are the culture and ethnic backgrounds of the members? What are their personalities? All of these components make up who the individual members of the teams are. The individual, of course, determine the interactions in the team and how they define who they are, how they will function, and how you as the intern will play a role in the team. They also determine how the team goes through the stages of group process, especially intimacy. If you don't know much about the culture or ethnicity of those represented in your agency (and specifically in your team), you may want to spend time now learning about these cultures or ethnicities, so that you have an appreciation of where people are coming from. You can do that by reading, talking to a fellow classmate who is of the same culture or ethnicity, or talking to your coworkers about their culture. This exercise may give you a greater awareness of that culture that helps make your interactions more meaningful and you a better social worker.

The NASW Code of Ethics in section 2.03 outlines the role of social workers on interdisciplinary teams.

> (a) Social workers who are members of an interdisciplinary team should participate in and contribute to decisions that affect the well-being of clients by drawing on the perspectives, values, and experiences of the social work profession. Professional and ethical obligations of the interdisciplinary team as a whole and of its individual members should be clearly established.

> (b) Social workers for whom a team decision raises ethical concerns should attempt to resolve the disagreement through appropriate channels. If the disagreement cannot be resolved, social workers should pursue other avenues to address their concerns consistent with client well-being.

Social workers have a status in the team in the agency. Depending on the setting of your field placement, social workers as a whole will have a status and reputation. Before we go on, take time as a class to discuss your opinions about how social workers are treated at your agency. Answer the following questions:

How the agency treats social workers

What type of agency are you placed in, and what is the reputation/status of social workers in the agency?

How are you treated as a social work intern?

Are there any BSWs there? Is there a difference between how BSWs and MSWs are treated?

If your internship experience is anything like what our students have felt, your reactions to the above questions will vary. Most of you will be observed and treated as who you are. But sometimes, especially where social workers are the minority (hospitals and schools), you may feel that you are the "low man on the totem pole," so to speak. We have had a social worker from a school district say she felt like the lone ranger hung out to dry because she tried to do something good for the students, had no support from anyone, and was the only social worker in the school. Another social worker who worked in a hospital said that she felt she was next to the janitor in order of importance on the staff and that sometimes even the janitor was more important.

Remember that many places need and require social workers, but because social workers are in the minority, they do not have a lot of support. For that reason your job becomes even more important. You alone possess the social work skills, resources, and knowledge base that are necessary to help the clients. In your mind, that should rank you as equal to the rest of the people in the agency. Unfortunately, the hospital, a traditional medical model, has always had a pecking order where doctors come first, followed by nurses, and so on. It would take a very special setting or a very mindful doctor to make the rest of the people feel equal.

It also becomes your responsibility as the newest member of the social work profession to represent the profession and your school appropriately. The more professional and proficient you are, the more respect the profession receives, and the better social workers' reputations will become. Nationally, social workers have a reputation of being "do gooders" and "bleeding hearts." We may have those traits among us, but we also have a unique set of skills, an individual knowledge base, and a profession that we all can be proud of and represent in a strong manner every chance we get. This will help eliminate stereotypes of social workers and show people what we are capable of and what we are worth to an agency and its client base.

Section 5 of the NASW Code of Ethics, "Social Workers' Ethical Responsibilities to the Social Work Profession," delineates standards for integrity of the profession (section 5.01) and evaluation and research (section 5.02). The section on integrity of the profession is very relevant to our discussion here.

(a) Social workers should work toward the maintenance and promotion of high standards of practice.

(b) Social workers should uphold and advance the values, ethics, knowledge, and mission of the profession. Social workers should protect, enhance, and improve the integrity of the profession through appropriate study and research, active discussion, and responsible criticism of the profession.

(c) Social workers should contribute time and professional expertise to activities that promote respect for the value, integrity, and competence of the social work profession. These activities may include teaching, research, consultation, service, legislative testimony, presentations in the community, and participation in their professional organizations.

(d) Social workers should contribute to the knowledge base of social work and share with colleagues their knowledge related to practice, research, and ethics. Social workers should seek to contribute to the profession's literature and to share their knowledge at professional meetings and conferences.

(e) Social workers should act to prevent the unauthorized and unqualified practice of social work.

Thoughts to ponder

How can you alter people's perception about stereotypes of social workers?

When you meet a new group of people professionally, how do you want them to perceive you? Are you representing yourself accurately?

Integration of other course material	
HBSE	How might your assessment of a client differ from that of another person on your team, such as a nurse, doctor, or teacher?
Policy	What are the legal mandates for social workers in your agency setting?
Practice	How many social work teams have you come across in your internship experiences? How are they the same? How are they different?
Research	What practice literature can you find either supporting or not supporting interdisciplinary teams?

Resources

University of Washington School of Medicine
http://eduserv.hscer.washington.edu/bioethics/topics/team.html

John A. Hartford Foundation
http://www.gitt.org/full_social_work.html

Center of Human Development and Disability, University of Washington
http://depts.washington.edu/lend/coresem/socialwork/6a.htm

National Association of Social Workers
http://www.naswdc.org/practice/adolescent_health/ah0303.pdf

 When have you needed to take a detour in field? How did this occur, how did you feel, and was it beneficial?

Chapter 12
Boundaries:
The Invisible Lines of Trust

The idea of boundaries has been part of your life as long as you can remember, but not always the word *boundaries*. Phrases like "come to my house," "that's my sweater," or "you're invading my space" indicate you are setting or acknowledging a boundary. Boundaries are the limits we place on another human being around physical, emotional, and mental space.

Boundaries are easier to understand when we think about the concept of physical space. Most of us have a comfort zone about how close we allow strangers to get to us. We have another zone for acquaintances, which might be a little closer to your person, and we have an even closer zone for family, friends, and loved ones. That space we allow people into is the boundary we establish. Usually it is not a physical boundary, yet a strange uncomfortable feeling comes over us if someone gets too close to us physically. That amount of space is different in every culture.

We have those same boundaries in terms of emotional space and mental space. We don't let everyone we meet know what we are thinking and feeling. We choose who to tell and share information with. These are personal boundaries, and we begin to establish those boundaries early on in our development. Throughout our development, we refine these boundaries by clarifying what feels right and setting limits with people. Sometimes we have help developing these boundaries because of laws and social rules. If you live in a house, you know where your property line is. Maybe your family has a rule about when the phone can be used or not used, (such as no calls during dinner or after 10 p.m.)

Why Is It Important to Have Boundaries?

Boundaries protect us, both physically and emotionally. They establish structure, create order in our lives, and give us clear indications of hierarchy. For example, parents have a particular role to fulfill, both with each other and with their children. If a parent crosses the parent-child boundary, we have physical abuse, sexual abuse, and many emotional problems. These problems often continue through generations, where boundaries are violated and the cycle of abuse continues. One of our tasks as a social worker is to help clients develop appropriate boundaries and teach them how to maintain those boundaries. Clients, like ourselves, learn boundaries through cultural and societal norms but usually have to maintain them without the support of that same society. It is expected that you will learn to recognize when you have violated boundaries.

Why Do Boundary Violations Occur?

Some people don't have clearly defined boundaries because of crisis, poor role modeling, or many other reasons. Most of you can probably recall experiences where a complete stranger tells you more than you wanted to know or should know. That person likely has poor boundaries or does not maintain boundaries.

Clients who have a hard time creating and maintaining appropriate boundaries include people who are considered vulnerable, impulsive, confused, alone, or isolated. Usually these people have low self-esteem and need to be validated. They may be very dependent or manipulative and probably have had some kind of childhood trauma that causes relationship difficulties. Clients are not responsible for maintaining the boundaries between themselves and their social workers, and they will test the boundaries and see how far they can go. It is a natural human instinct. Do you remember having a substitute teacher in grade school or high school and telling the substitute lies, like "we already did that," or "we don't get homework"? That is testing the limits. That is also what clients will do, it is what happens in all new relationships, and it is how we know where we stand.

So if it is normal for a client to test the limits and test boundaries, then it is the social worker's responsibility to maintain the boundary. Sometimes it is hard for the social worker for several reasons. Sometimes the social worker is so stressed or burned-out that it is hard to maintain the boundaries. Maintaining boundaries takes work, and you must be actively thinking about your interactions with your clients. As students, more likely than not, the reason you may have difficulty maintaining boundaries is inexperience. You are new to the field and are accustomed to spending time with people developing and maintaining other types of relationships. You will now be clarifying, developing, maintaining, and reinforcing professional boundaries. Be patient, as it will take practice.

Often, as social workers, we are helping our clients do the same things with their boundaries. In order to teach them to effectively manage their boundaries, you need to model appropriate boundaries—both personal and professional. It is important to define these boundaries and understand why they are needed. Professional boundaries exist to protect the social worker and the client. They put limits on the relationship, which helps the client feel safe. Professional boundaries also frame the role(s) the social worker will take on.

The first set of boundaries consists of explaining the rules of treatment: how often it will occur, when it will occur, how long it will take, how much it will cost, and what the expected outcome is. These preliminary boundaries set the tone for how the relationship will develop between you and the client. They create a safe space and allow the client to develop trust. There may be other boundaries that your agency or program overlay on this relationship as well, like who to contact in an emergency, and what constitutes an emergency. Boundaries are established to make sure that the client's best interests are being considered. Boundaries also support the relationship that forms between the client and the social worker, protecting and guarding them both.

When you enter into a relationship as a social worker with a client, you need to understand that the relationship is uneven in terms of power. As a professional, you have a knowledge base and experience that your client does not have. You become the expert in the room because of your knowledge, because it is your office space, and because you are in charge of what happens. This power differential makes you responsible for what happens in the agency between you and the client. That power differential makes you responsible for the boundaries of the relationship.

Thoughts to ponder

What do you think of the power differential between you and your client?

Are there ways to decrease the inequality?

Would you want to change the power differential? Why or why not? In what settings would it be good to balance the power and where would it not be good?

Boundary violations can be divided into categories. Here we will discuss sexual boundaries, other physical contact, overfamiliarity, personal gain, gift giving, treating family and friends, and social contact. These categories were delineated by The College of Psychologists of Ontario in 1998.

Sexual Boundaries

When researching professional boundaries in the social work literature, almost everything you find is focused on sexual boundaries and preventing sexual encounters with clients, including sexual harassment. The rule on sexual contact with clients is really simple to state, but apparently difficult for some to adhere to: there is *no sexual contact of any kind* for any reason with clients. Sexual contact includes intercourse, kissing, flirting, inappropriate conversation, or requiring sexual favors in exchange for treatment. The NASW Code of Ethics is very clear about sexual relationships (section 1.09).

> (a) Social workers should under no circumstances engage in sexual activities or sexual contact with current clients, whether such contact is consensual or forced.

(b) Social workers should not engage in sexual activities or sexual contact with clients' relatives or other individuals with whom clients maintain a close personal relationship when there is a risk of exploitation or potential harm to the client.... Social workers—not their clients, their clients' relatives, or other individuals with whom the client maintains a personal relationship—assume the full burden for setting clear, appropriate, and culturally sensitive boundaries.

(c) Social workers should not engage in sexual activities or sexual contact with former clients.

(d) Social workers should not provide clinical services to individuals with whom they have had a prior sexual relationship.

Other Physical Contact

Some touching of clients needs further elaboration besides a blanket rule of NO. This touching includes comforting someone who is crying in your office. A natural instinct for some social workers might include a hug, hand-holding, or a pat on the shoulder. All of these would be appropriate if they met the following criteria: (1) you have asked the client's permission first, (2) your intentions are only momentary comfort, and (3) the client is clear about your intentions. These criteria are important, because then there is no misunderstanding about what occurred. Something important to note here is that many times our clients have a history of boundary violations that could involve sexual abuse, rape, sexual harassment, and domestic violence. An unexpected or unwanted touch, no matter how well-intentioned, may violate their boundaries and ruin the relationship that could help others heal: the relationship with you, the social worker.

Another population, little children, may want you to touch them all the time, for example, getting a hug every morning when they come to see you. Make sure that the children and the caretakers are OK with it, that your intentions are clear, and that the child knows what you are doing. Again, the child might have been abused, and your touching him or her, although well meaning, could cause anxiety and fear. For example, for a child with a cold who is crying, you might naturally take a tissue to help them blow their nose and wipe their eyes. Yet if someone once tried to suffocate this child, your innocent and helpful act could trigger some very sensitive memories, making things worse for the client. Remember, physical boundaries are very delicate and are the first layer of defense mechanisms that some clients may have established for good reasons.

Once again, the NASW Code of Ethics speaks to this type of situation.

Social workers should not engage in physical contact with clients when there is a possibility of psychological harm to the client as a result of the contact (such as cradling or caressing clients). Social workers who engage in appropriate physical contact with clients are responsible for setting clear, appropriate, and culturally sensitive boundaries that govern such physical contact. (section 1.10)

Overfamiliarity

The remaining boundary issues—overfamiliarity, personal gain, gift giving, treating family and friends, and social contact—are not as clear as the rules on sexual contact. Sometimes these areas do not have definitive answers, but we will explain each one to help you understand these different boundary areas.

When discussing overfamiliarity, we include things like discussing topics that have no relation to the issue the client is seeing you about. For instance, your client is a teenager who sees you to discuss problems in school, and you spend time talking about how much his or her parents make and the type of car that they drive. Or your client is an elderly woman on a fixed income who can't afford her medicine, and you discuss instead how your parents grew up in the same neighborhood that she did. Another form of overfamiliarity is, having known the client for a long time, you start assuming you know why he or she acted in a certain way, which may stop communication or cause a power struggle over who is right.

Personal Gain

Another boundary violation is personal gain. For instance, your client works at a clothing store and offers you their discount if you buy clothes at the store. Or your client works at a movie theater and offers to let you see movies for free. Clients have those perks from jobs for themselves and maybe family members (depending on how the benefits are explained to them). You cannot exploit that benefit because you will put the client in an uncomfortable place.

Personal gain can also crop up when you take a client's case only because it will benefit you, make you look good, get you a promotion at work, or be a case to publish in a presentation or a journal article. One real example that we know of involved a client who owned an automotive detailing shop. He offered his social worker a huge discount on the detailing of his car. The social worker accepted the discount, and while the car was being detailed, the client requested longer sessions and wanted to pay less for those sessions. It is awkward to barter with your social worker. How difficult would it have been if the social worker's car had been stolen while it was being detailed? It could make it impossible to be objective in helping the client, no matter how hard the social worker tried.

Conflicts of interest like those mentioned above are covered by the Code of Ethics in section 1.06.

(a) Social workers should be alert to and avoid conflicts of interest that interfere with the exercise of professional discretion and impartial judgment.

(b) Social workers should not take unfair advantage of any professional relationship or exploit others to further their personal, religious, political, or business interests.

(c) Social workers should not engage in dual or multiple relationships with clients or former clients in which there is a risk of exploitation or potential harm to the client.

(d) When social workers provide services to two or more people who have a relationship with each other (for example, couples, family members), social workers should clarify with all parties which individuals will be considered clients and the nature of social workers' professional obligations to the various individuals who are receiving services.

Gift Giving

According to the NASW Code of Ethics, we as social workers cannot accept gifts from clients. Section 1.13, "Payment for Services" states: "Social workers should avoid accepting goods or services from clients as payment for professional service." Accepting gifts for what we do in our capacity as social workers is awkward and creates many unanswered questions. What if you didn't like the gift? What if you feel obligated to give the client a gift? Does it mean that you should offer more services, better services, or discounted services because of the gift? Does the client think that he or she is better than other clients now or feel we owe him or her special considerations? The idea of gift-giving from a client to a social worker has been deemed inappropriate by the Code of Ethics because of all the potential problems, but it also presents a few ambiguities. What if you are working with a child who brings you a stuffed animal for your office or some Halloween candy after he or she went trick-or-treating? Learning to share and trust you enough to want to give you a gift may be significant in the child's treatment process, and refusing the gift may impede progress. When this occurs, it is one of those gray areas in ethics, and you should discuss it with your supervisor.

Thoughts to ponder

How would you tell a client you cannot accept a gift without hurting his or her feelings or jeopardizing the relationship?

There will come a time when you are offered a gift by a client for the assistance you gave them. Clients who are from other cultures may want to give you a token of their appreciation—perhaps something they baked, an item from their country, or some other acknowledgment of your work. You must use your best cultural sensitivity in these cases, as refusing the gift could be quite offensive to your client.

Treating Family and Friends

A clear boundary violation is offering to treat family and friends. One of the first things taught in social work classes is not to try social work with any of your family members. Family roles and systems are constantly trying to maintain homeostasis without adding any unnecessary new roles to the system. Besides, as a social worker and a family member, the issues are too close to your heart and you can't offer the objectivity that is so needed and expected when you are a social worker. An example might arise if a doctor suggests that your sick parent sign a living will. As an adult child, if you are not ready for your parent to sign a living will (an order of do not resuscitate), you might not hear what your parent wants and might not be able to take the role of social worker in conversation with your family members, because of your emotional involvement.

Similar things could be said about friends. There are things you may need to say as a social worker that you can't say as a friend. For instance, a friend may have a serious drug problem, and you are concerned. If you confront as a social worker and offer treatment options, the friend may see you as a betrayer, because you knew about the drug use only because of your friendship. Your friend may feel that you violated his or her trust, and may never again talk to you as a friend, and may not want to see a social worker either.

Social Contact

The last area where boundary violations tend to occur is in social contact. This is probably the grayest area of all, especially if you live in the community that you work in. Social contact involves any contact with clients outside the social work relationship, like using their business for something, serving on committees together, or seeing each other socially. Perhaps your children and your client's children go to the same school, and you and your client both want to be active members of the Parent-Teacher Association (PTA), or maybe you and your client attend the same twelve-step meeting for Alcoholics Anonymous.

On the surface this sounds harmless. However, further examination turns up some problems. What happens if the PTA makes a strong stand to change the school rule requiring that children all wear uniforms. You disagree with the idea, but your client is spearheading the initiative. How would you keep your social work/client relationship separate from the adversarial role on the PTA issue? Likewise, what if your favorite clothing store somehow confuses a major special order for you or loses your layaway but refuses to reimburse you for your loss, and your client is the one refusing to give you back your money? You may need to sue to get your money back. How does that work in your relationship with your client in your capacity as a social worker? These are awkward situations, and best avoided.

Whenever possible, especially in very large metropolitan areas, try not to live in the area that you work. When this is not possible, make your connections in the community clear and businesslike. You will probably run into clients all the time outside of your agency setting, so be polite and friendly, but distant. When faced with more than a social work relationship with a client, try to keep it at a minimum, don't initiate anything more than what is expected in that setting, and acknowledge the awkwardness with the client from the beginning, so that you can talk about avoiding difficulty in the future. It is always best to let your clients know how you will greet them in public before it happens the first time. They will then know what to expect.

Signs That a Boundary Violation Is Occurring

As a social worker you are responsible for maintaining the professional boundaries. The best way to do this is to constantly assess your practice both independently and with your supervisor. You can ask yourself questions about your relationship with the client to assure yourself that the boundaries are intact. Boundaries generally erode slowly; sometimes it is not very obvious, so look at the relationship from the beginning to the present when assessing the change. Are you still objective? Can you see both sides of the issue and understand where the client is incorrect or losing his or her own objectivity? Are you treating that client as special or different? Is it OK that he or she is late or doesn't have to be responsible for his or her actions? Do you allow that client to do things that you wouldn't let other clients do? If so, these are all signs that the boundaries are becoming diffuse or cloudy. Have you disclosed information to this client about other clients? Maybe it's not even a name but information about their case, like "I had another client go through the same thing as you" and similar situations. This is of course inappropriate and borders on breaking confidentiality.

It is really not hard for clients to learn about who is being treated by whom and for what. You think an agency is an anonymous place, but most agencies are just a microcosm of where we live. Clients know each other and talk to one another, when we as social workers can't. Most social workers and agencies rely on word of mouth for referral, and clients will share conversations frequently. Wouldn't it be awful if a client said to a friend, "My social worker is treating someone who did blah, blah, blah" and the second person recognized his or her own story?

Finally, you know you are getting too close to a client when you start self-disclosing. Clients should know little about you, if anything. Self-disclosure can be one of the hardest areas to define. It can be hard to be a social worker without having some ability to self-disclose in professional use of self. When you use humor correctly in a session, it's good use of self—but it also shows you have a sense of humor. When you say to a child, "My favorite ice cream is vanilla too," that boundary is self-disclosure but is not inherently harmful. When discussing self-disclosure as a bonding issue, you are using the session to share that you have had similar problems or that you are concerned about this situation because of what you went through. That type of self-disclosure changes you from a social worker providing services to a person sharing his or her problem with another person. Once boundaries are gone, they are difficult to restore, and you may have lost the therapeutic relationship you had.

If in your self-analysis any of these issues come up, make sure you discuss them in supervision. These signs are clues that boundaries are being violated and that you need assistance in reestablishing them.

Consequences of Boundary Violation

The consequences of boundary violations vary. Sometimes you can apologize for them, boundaries can be clarified and reinforced, and it is OK. Sometimes, especially when violations are frequent or severe, there are consequences to both the social worker and the client.

For the client, becoming dependent on the worker can immobilize the client, or even cause regression. The client may mistrust and feel unsafe with that social worker (and maybe with the entire helping profession), preventing the client from seeking help and causing more difficulties in his or her life. For the social worker, boundary violations can ruin his or her career. If a client feels violated and shares that feeling with other people in the agency or community, how likely is it that anyone else will go to that worker? If the boundary violation is serious enough, a social worker's license can be revoked or suspended, leaving the social worker without the ability to work.

Other Boundaries

This chapter started out discussing boundaries as a general concept and a part of all relationships. But most of this chapter has been a delineation of boundaries between social workers and clients. There are other boundaries that as a student you must be aware of, between you and your teacher, you and your supervisor, and you and your coworkers. Your teacher and your supervisor are mostly responsible for maintaining those boundaries, and you and your coworkers are equally responsible for your relationship. But if a teacher or supervisor breaks a boundary, especially in the context of sex, take all necessary action to address the issue, bringing in other people if you have to.

The best way to maintain boundaries is to be clear about what they are from the beginning. Know what the expectations are about dress code, for instance. In residential settings for kids, you may be expected to dress ready to play or restrain, but that doesn't mean your torn jeans or your shirt with one arm or no back is appropriate. Clothing in most settings will tell you who are staff and who are the clients. Other things to consider are the boundaries for e-mails and phone calls. What is appropriate to discuss in the office and what is not?

The same type of questions can be asked about your professor. They include boundaries regarding assignments and class attendance. Is your teacher firm about assignment deadlines? Do you know who will be flexible and when?

Expect that maintaining boundaries takes as much work as establishing relationships. Sometimes you don't know if you are crossing a boundary until it's too late. Keeping watch on your boundaries is a way of maintaining relationships and keeping them healthy within the appropriate context (e.g., a friend/friend relationship or a social work/client relationship). When establishing boundaries, it is always a good idea to have firm, clear boundaries with people first. Once the relationship is established, it is easy to make them a little closer and more flexible. It is always harder to start with really flexible, close boundaries and have to establish firmer boundaries. Most people, including clients, will have a hard time understanding why the boundaries changed from flexible and close to rigid and distant.

Integration of other course material

HBSE   How can you determine what the formal and informal boundaries are in a community?

Policy   What are the options available to a client if a boundary violation occurs?

Practice   What strategies can you think of to help you develop and maintain appropriate professional boundaries with your clients?

Research   What does the research show regarding how often boundary violations occur and in what areas?

Resources

The College of Psychologists of Ontario
http://www.cpo.on.ca/Bulletin/Selected%20Articles/Professional%20Boundaries.htm

New York State Office of the Professions
http://www.op.nysed.gov/swboundaries.htm

```
┌──────────┐
│          │
│    NO    │
│ DUMPING  │
│ ALLOWED  │
│          │
└──────────┘
```

Ever feel taken advantage of in your internship? When did this happen? Describe the circumstances, how you felt, and what you did about it.

Did you speak with your supervisor? Why or why not?

Chapter 13
Difficult Issues and Difficult Clients

What can we write that would help you through difficult issues that you will face or difficult cases that you will need to work out for your clients? Each of us will find different aspects of social work more appealing and more exciting than others. For instance, one of the authors of this book likes clinical work with drug-addicted and alcoholic adolescents. The other author would prefer to organize a union around workplace-safety issues or to increase the awareness of social work issues internationally. Although we respect each other's differences and are both trained to do either job, we choose to specialize in particular areas because of our interests.

The point is that throughout your career each of you will define for yourself what a difficult issue or population is for you to work with. Our intention in this chapter is to explore issues that come up frequently for students in their fieldwork, so that you may know what to expect. The common issues that always seem to come up are

conflicts between personal and agency values;

use of alternative methods, techniques, or skills to work with clients;

transference and countertransference;

recognizing when you, the social worker, are being difficult;

working within your own community;

negotiating collaborative agreements between a variety of agencies and communities;

chronic psychiatric impairments of individual clients or their family members;

the reluctant or resistant client; and

disapproval of how other colleagues treat clients.

Ethical Conflicts

In each chapter of this book we have pointed out the section from the NASW Code of Ethics that has some bearing on the content of the chapter. The Code of Ethics is a very useful tool that you should keep readily available. You can purchase the code in booklet form from NASW, and it is probably also in a number of your text books (including this one; see appendix A), or it can be easily downloaded or bookmarked on the internet. The Code of Ethics started out as a very short document (less than two pages) and over the years has increased in depth and breadth, especially in areas that were vague or in areas where new issues arose. Although the code tries to be inclusive, there is no way that it can cover every issue that arises in social work practice. Our suggestion is to start with the Code of Ethics when struggling with an issue, and hopefully it will give you guidance.

Sometimes the code cannot give an answer because your problem is too vague or too specific. Several social work ethicists, such as Elaine Congress and Fredric Reamer, have spent a large part of their careers looking at ethical dilemmas and trying to provide guidance to social work practitioners and educators on how to best approach difficult issues. Unfortunately for you as a new social worker, the dilemmas faced by social workers do not always have clear-cut answers. Ethical dilemmas are rarely black and white—there is so much gray area associated with ethical issues. In fact, when attending training or classes on ethics, you will often walk out with more questions than you walked in with!

One of the models designed to help you sort out ethical dilemmas comes from Congress in her book *Social Work Values and Ethics* (1999). It uses the acronym ETHIC to help you remember how to sort out your choices.

E   Examine relevant personal, societal, agency, client, and professional values.

T   Think about what ethical standard of the NASW Code of Ethics applies to the situation, as well as other laws and case decisions.

H   Hypothesize about possible consequences of different decisions.

I   Identify who will benefit and who will be harmed in view of social work's commitment to the most vulnerable.

C   Consult with supervisors and colleagues about the most ethical choice.

After consulting the Code of Ethics, if the answer to your question is unclear or unsatisfactory, you can always consult colleagues and your supervisor. We must warn you, however, that each social worker is an individual, and you may end up with as many answers as people that you asked. The dialogue that takes place will usually help you clarify your response. Together, you and your colleagues can usually come up with a solution that all can live with, by selecting components of many ideas and forming one direction to pursue.

Conflicts between Personal and Agency Values

Ethics become an issue when your personal values come into direct conflict with professional boundaries. This usually occurs when a client makes a choice, under the guise of self-determination, to do something that is in direct violation of your own values. This personal and professional dilemma can also occur at the macrolevel when you disagree with a decision your agency has made. An obvious microlevel example of this is when a client decides to get an abortion and your personal belief is that abortions are wrong. A macrolevel example is if an organizational decision is made by your agency, a drug treatment program, to start a needle-exchange program to minimize the risk of HIV. You don't believe that those programs are a good idea because you think that needle-exchange programs encourage the same drug use that you are trying to treat. These scenarios highlight a difference in values between you and your client or you and your agency. You have several options to pursue while you try to sort out where you stand on these dilemmas.

The first is to say nothing, regardless of your feelings, and let the agency and your client choose to do what they want. This sounds easy, but it entails that you put your personal values aside, and this decision may come back again and again. It could make working in your agency uncomfortable. Your second choice is to ask questions and provide information on the pros and cons of the decision, so that your client and your agency are sure they made the right decision and that you have raised your awareness of other viewpoints on the issue. It is very inappropriate to force a client to change his or her mind. But it is your responsibility to be sure the client has all the facts and has sorted out all feelings regarding his or her decision before acting on it. It is appropriate to discuss with your agency administrators their stance on an issue. Be aware that challenging agency policy may make you unpopular, and it could become difficult to work there—the agency attitude toward change and resistance to change will affect how you are perceived if you do this. It could, however, make you well respected and regarded as an up-and-coming leader in the agency if your points are well taken and change people's minds.

Your third option is to seek supervision and reflect on why you feel the way you do. Sometimes talking out loud with another person can clarify your stance and the origin of that opinion or value. Individual reflection can also help. Ask yourself, Where does my value come from? Do I believe that for myself, or is it a value I carry from my parents that I have not questioned? Or is it a value I acquired somewhere else (e.g., religion or former community) that I have not fully discerned and need to rethink? These types of questions are not easy but are essential in the realm of ethical decision making. While you are still a student, you can use a teacher or your peers for this discernment process.

Your final option is to refuse to work with that client or for that agency any longer. If you cannot set aside your personal values and you feel uncomfortable with your or the agency's actions, it may be time to move on. Recognize the reason that you can't change your values and be sure to clearly and thoroughly research the next agency you go to. You will have to explain to a new employer what type of issues you cannot work with or what conditions you cannot work under. Remember, this could limit the places you can work and the supervisors who are willing to give you a chance within their agencies. In the end, you have to be comfortable and confident wherever you work.

Thoughts to ponder

How do you make your decisions?

Do you have values that you adopted because they were your parents' and that you no longer feel as strongly about as when you were taught them?

Have you had any ethical dilemmas in the field? If so, what did you do to resolve them? If you haven't had any yet, do you anticipate any such issues?

Use of Alternative Methods

Another set of difficult issues that we believe to be problematic for students is the use of alternative techniques to deal with clients. In your classes, both in psychology and social work, you will be exposed to many theories and techniques. The ones you will use with clients are the theories and skills that you practice in class and that your supervisor has competence in, so he or she can guide you.

The longer you are in the field, the more opportunities you will have to receive specialized training in other areas. The longer you are in the field, the more you will see clients who will not respond to the skills and theories you have learned thus far. There are many other techniques and skills being taught to advance your level of practice. Treatment approaches such as hypnotism, eye movement desensitization and reprocessing (EMDR), rapid eye movement (REM), and rebirthing are techniques that many people receive specialized training in. Just as now you explain to your clients that you are an intern, you must also explain to your clients when you are practicing a new technique or method. For ethical reasons you need to tell clients that you are doing something new and that you are unsure how it will be as an experience for you or them. It is expected that if you are trying something new with a client, you have been properly trained and you feel confident that you can successfully complete the tasks that are part of the new technique.

If your teacher discusses a new technique in class that you want to try now, check it with your supervisor. Make sure he or she is aware of what you want to do, why you think it will work, and if it fits the therapeutic milieu of the agency. Make sure your supervisor or someone else knows the technique, in case you need help. There is something known as best practice with clients: best practices are well researched and are known to work for that specific client group or problem. Many people in your agency will know about best practices and be able to help you with the technique or theory.

Transference and Countertransference

Transference and countertransference can be difficult for new social workers. Transference is when clients associate the social worker with someone in their life and start treating the social worker like that person, sometimes negatively, sometimes positively. Countertransference is the same thing for the social worker, who associates the client with someone else. It is the reverse of transference.

When the issue occurs in your practice as a social worker, it may not be obvious right away. You may feel like the relationship is not building as fast as most of your client-worker relationships, or it just feels like it's not working and you are not sure what is happening. You need to reflect on your practice by yourself and with your supervisor to determine why this relationship is not working. Chances are good that countertransference or transference is getting in the way. Once made aware that this is the issue, you can address it fairly easily. If it is your issue, talk about it in supervision and adjust your behavior accordingly with your client.

If it is your clients' issue, try to explore with them who you might be reminding them of. Identifying the transference will allow the client the opportunity to resolve any issues that remain about that relationship. Transference becomes a problem only when it's not identified. Used appropriately, it can assist clients and help them make great strides in their treatment.

Recognizing When You Are Being Difficult

As well as being a social worker, you are also a human being who has personality quirks that will occasionally get in the way of your work. This is not the same as transference because it has nothing to do with your interaction with the client. Instead, it is an area of life that impedes your work as a social worker. An example of this may be that you are a morning person, very energetic and cheerful as soon as you wake up. You know that your down time is late afternoon, but you are working in a school-based youth service program where you see most clients after school. As you may know, most adolescents are not morning people and may just be waking up after school! A client who is half asleep may find your energy level very unpleasant in the morning, and because you are tired in the afternoon, you may find it difficult to engage a client in meaningful conversation. It is easy to report, "Client was quiet and did not engage in meaningful conversation," making it appear that it is the client's problem. Your responsibility as the social worker is to assess your part in the relationship and see what you can do to alter it. Acknowledging the problem and putting the onus on the client is irresponsible.

Another example would be if you made culturally insensitive comments to a client and they stopped talking to you. Labeling that client as unresponsive or reluctant puts the responsibility on the client, when you should understand the difficulty is on your end.

Working within Your Own Community

The fourth area that causes some difficulty for many students is working within their own community. We already mentioned problems with this when we discussed boundaries in chapter 12. The main issue is how much self-disclosure is comfortable for you. When you live in the community where you work, people know a lot about you. They will see you shopping, going out to dinner, attending church, and visiting your child's school. Some social workers also feel awkward about the dual relationships that can occur as we discussed previously (e.g., your child playing with the child of your client). It is better to avoid these situations whenever possible. If you are in a position where you must live and work in the same community, set up boundaries that will help clients understand when to approach you about work issues and when you are not on duty. Monitor those boundaries carefully on a fairly regular basis. This protects you from burnout and stress and protects clients from awkward moments as well.

Negotiation with Other Agencies

Another area of difficulty for many social workers is negotiating collaborative agreements among agencies. As funding gets cut and as our world seems to get smaller and smaller, it becomes ever more necessary for all of us to work together to assist everyone. Many agencies within a community are working on similar issues and maybe even with similar clients. To be the most effective and efficient, many agencies are now working together and hiring consultants to do pieces of their program (e.g., evaluation).

When agencies decide to collaborate, a social worker usually brokers the deal. This includes negotiating the various components of the program. For example, who will be the lead agency? The lead agency usually receives the funding and is ultimately responsible for the program. Which agency will provide the evaluation? Which agency will design and implement the different segments of the program? There are a lot of pieces to negotiate and whether the agencies will work together well depends on how firmly established the relationships are between the agencies. The social worker that leads this effort will be responsible for keeping communication lines open, keeping track of the tasks and responsibilities of each agency, and overseeing everyone's accountability to the project. If you ever have this task, be clear, open, and honest with everyone. The job is much less stressful when everyone is doing his or her share and everyone is reliable. It becomes difficult when some are not always honest—the agencies involved want their funds but do not always want to produce the work to the agreed quality, or are unable to produce the work for other reasons. When this occurs you need to scramble to get all the tasks done, and it causes strained relations.

A similar situation can arise in a group project for class. We are sure that at some point you have been in a group where another student did not fulfill his or her piece of the project in the specified amount of time. Or maybe it was in on time but was not the quality the group expected. Someone has to step forward to tell the person the problem and to correct the situation. Afterward, because the class is still going on, you need to continue to get along. So not only is the negotiation important, but so is the relationship building and the leadership used to get the agencies to work together. Remember, open, clear, and honest communication will see you through.

Chronic Psychiatric Impairments

Another difficulty faced by social workers is when the client or the client's family members have mental health issues. Not all social workers choose to work in mental health. At the bachelor's level you probably receive little classroom education on the topic of mental health unless you choose to take an abnormal psychology class. Just because your career path is not in mental health does not mean that you will not come across the issue. Many clients who are in social work settings have multiple issues, and some may very well have mental health issues. It is important for you to have a general understanding of diagnosis and medications. When you take a complete biopsychosocial, ask about the client's mental health history and the family's relevant history. You, as the social worker, should be familiar enough with the DSM-IV-TR to learn about the criteria for a diagnosis and what types of medicine clients are taking.

As you continue to work with your clients, you will be able to observe if they are following treatment. You will also be able to tell when they may be having difficulty and need assistance. When the general population thinks about mental health issues, there is a general fear for their own safety. As social workers you need to be aware that most people with mental illness are not a danger. If they are having a difficult day, they are probably more a danger to themselves than to others. As a responsible student, and soon to be social worker, we encourage you to become familiar with diagnoses like depression, bipolar disorder, and schizophrenia. Recognize the obstacles your clients may be facing, and assist them within your scope of practice the best you know how, with encouragement, support, and education as needed from your supervisor.

The Reluctant or Resistant Client

Depending on where you work, you may meet clients that do not necessarily want the services your agency provides. You may be at a nursing home where clients don't want to be there but cannot care for themselves at home and have no one else to care for them. You may work in a drug and alcohol rehabilitation program where a judge has assigned a client to complete a drug program or go to jail instead, and the client does not believe he or she has a drug problem. These clients are known as involuntary, reluctant, or resistant and appear in many agencies in various ways fairly frequently. These clients can be harder to engage, get to know, and help. There is a good chance they will refuse to talk to you. Your challenge is to break through that barrier and provide the care that your client needs and you want to give. There are semester-long courses spent on how to assist this type of client; here we can only suggest to keep trying. Your perseverance will not go unnoticed and often will be all it takes to persuade the person to speak. Another idea is to give clients time and space to get used to the idea that they have no choice about being here and that it is not as bad as they thought or that they are going to make the best of the situation. You will need to try a variety of techniques and be patient.

Disapproval of Colleagues' Treatment of Clients

The final area social work students have told us can be difficult is when they disapprove of how another colleague treats clients. It is our teaching and belief that all people, not just clients, should be treated with respect and dignity as human beings. So it doesn't matter what setting we are in; it matters that care and compassion are present in our dealings with others. Not everyone holds that belief, however, even some people in the helping profession. When students experience this in the field, we try to do a variety of things. The first is to educate students that not everyone has the same underlying principles about basic human rights, or sometimes people may be so burned out that they treat clients with disdain or disrespect. Your coworker may also be so burned out or fed up with a client population or a particular client that he or she has difficulty being patient and respectful. This issue needs to be addressed.

When students see inappropriate treatment of clients, we encourage them to talk to their coworker about it. We recognize it is not easy to confront colleagues about how they are working or treating clients. But before you go over their head and talk to your supervisor, your colleague needs a chance to give his or her point of view. We never really know what is happening with another person—there could be medical problems, personal issues, difficulties at home, and so on. Your colleagues are under no obligation to tell you all their private affairs, but by speaking with them first, you allow them to speak up and to see how others perceive their actions.

If things do not improve, you may be forced to report the incidents to your supervisor. It is important that the situation change, and if you have knowledge of a problem, especially regarding the treatment of clients, you have a responsibility to address it. If the person is burned out, you might encourage them to take vacation time or a different job. Help your coworker, and don't make problems worse by not acknowledging them.

We could have spent weeks of the semester on each type of difficult issue and probably added some new topics as well. This is not a comprehensive explanation or an exhaustive list of the issues you may face in this profession. We can say with confidence that the longer you are in the field, the more knowledge and experience you will have to address these issues. Hopefully you won't see difficult issues constantly in your daily routine as a social worker. You may even get to the point where you see difficult issues as challenges that can be faced in a positive way.

Integration of other course material

HBSE	During the assessment process with a client, is there anything you could do to anticipate and alleviate any difficulties that you might encounter?
Policy	What is your agency policy regarding how to handle difficult situations with clients?
Practice	What is the benefit to your practice as a social worker of having difficult practice issues?
Research	Is there a research project you could set up to determine, when there is difficulty between social worker and client, how often this difficulty lies with the social worker?

Resources

National Mental Health Association
http://www.nmha.org/

Behavioral Science Consultants on Ethics
http://hometown.aol.com/egeratylsw/ethics.html

Value Conflicts
http://www.socialworker.com/jswve/

Transference and Countertransference
http://www.crisiscounseling.com/Articles/Transference.htm
http://www.ishhr.org/conference/articles/tienhoven.pdf

 **Ethical dilemmas are prevalent throughout the field internship experience. Take a moment to process an ethical question or dilemma you were faced with.**

Describe the ethical dilemma or question.

Who did you turn to for help?

What happened?

Did you follow any particular ethical decision-making model? Which one? How did it work?

Chapter 14
Self-Evaluation

Guess what? You are coming into the home stretch! Only a few weeks left and you'll have finished the semester! For some of you, it may mean you are done with field completely; others might have another semester or two. Whatever the case, we are sure that you have been exposed to many new situations where you have been able to do things that you would not have believed possible when you declared yourself to be a social work major. Now it is time to reflect on your experience over the semester and see what you have accomplished, and how far you have come in your professional development. In other words, it is time for self-evaluation.

For many of you, your internship was your first professional work experience. That means you are about to have your first evaluation. Work evaluations are done on multiple levels—there is usually a 90-day probationary period for all employees, and if you pass that, you will have an annual review. The annual review is much like your field evaluation. It can include personal work ethics, your competency, how you fit into the agency's work culture, and your effectiveness with clients and staff. We will take a look at what this all means in a moment.

Many of you have had jobs before. Whether they were in the field of social work or not, you probably had a performance appraisal. Maybe this appraisal was informal (Hey, you are doing a great job!), or formal, where you sat down and signed an evaluation. Your field evaluation will be similar in many respects, because it is time to receive feedback.

We would like you to evaluate *yourself* before your supervisor evaluates you. In order to do this, you will need some materials. Gather your journal, your contract, your chapter 1 exercise about preparing your agency contract, and the blank evaluation used by your social work program or the agency you are at. Spend time reviewing these materials. You'll use them as we discuss work expectations and evaluation. First, we'll discuss your personal inventory.

Work Ethic

You are probably familiar with what has been called the "Protestant work ethic," which encompasses commitment, hard work, loyalty, dedication, passion, and self-sacrifice. Most employers still expect hard work and commitment, but the work force has changed. People are not willing to sacrifice themselves for their employers. Workers' loyalty has changed because their sense is that organizations are not loyal now, due to downsizing, layoffs, closures, and mergers. Permanent employment is not guaranteed, and employees never know how long the job will be there.

We'd like to contend that all the pieces of the Protestant work ethic still need to exist for you as an employee, as a human being. While at your job, for your own career development, you need to be hard-working, committed, loyal, and dedicated. For those who have never worked or who have worked only in temporary jobs, we'd like to take a few moments to operationalize those words. Take some time to answer these questions.

Work ethic

What does it mean to be a good employee?

What personal qualities do employers look for when hiring someone?

What personal qualities do employers look for when promoting someone?

What are things you should not do because they will get you in trouble at work?

Share your answers in small groups and see what similarities exist.

Does your list include any of the following things?

Punctuality

Following the dress code

Making sure your cell phone is off

Not checking your personal e-mail while at the office

Not taking off every possible minute of time as soon as you earn it

These are just a few examples of things to be aware of when thinking about working hard and doing a good job. One of us worked for a social work agency that was a real stickler for promptness. At that place a 9 a.m. start time meant 9:00 at your desk, already having your coffee and having been to the restroom. One employee was fired because she couldn't get to work by 9:00, even though she stayed almost every night past 6:00 and got all her work done.

Some way to understand what employers look for in an employee is to work everyday as though you are the owner or director of the agency. Short-term hard work, dedication, commitment, and positive attitude will get you far. Building your abilities, your knowledge, and your reputation, you will be ready to handle most other jobs later in your career. If you are willing to work in a team, a strong communicator, intrinsically motivated (motivated inside yourself, not outside by money or fear or punishment), productive, prepared, organized, and dependable, you have the essential qualities that will help you go far in your career.

Here are some work habits that are frowned upon.

Packed up and work area organized to leave before quitting time, with you watching the clock

Not following the dress code

Being late

Forgetting to share information

Acting as an individual, not as a team member

Using company resources for personal use—computers, copiers, fax machines, postage machines, etc.

Inappropriate language (cursing, swearing, gossiping)

Making personal calls from your office

Here are some work habits that will benefit your career and make you invaluable to any agency.

Being prepared to work until the job is done

Taking on additional responsibilities

Being creative

Pointing out problems only when you can also give solutions

Showing respect

Being dependable and reliable

Being responsible for the work of the organization, not just your work within the team

Having a positive attitude

Perhaps you already have good work habits, developed at your first job at the local mall or when you baby-sat. If this is the first time you are reading about developing a work ethic, be sure you understand it thoroughly and incorporate it as your own. Not everyone has this work ethic, and they will lose out through their work experience and you will benefit. As you enter the profession, ignore what others do, because it may be against your career goals and the work ethic you are building. It may frustrate you when you believe you are working very hard and others are not doing their part. You will benefit later on, as you are looking at long-term gain and the benefit for your clients. You also need to keep in mind that you do have a personal life and need to balance it appropriately with your work ethic. You also must be careful that you are not doing more than you should for clients; they need to become independent, not look to you to do everything for them.

The traits discussed above are the first level of evaluation that your supervisor will make prior to looking at your social work skills or the individual points on your individual contract or job description. So this is where we will start in your own evaluation. Your personal inventory is critical to successful employment in any field.

Thoughts to ponder

What can you say about your own work ethic?

Where can you improve your work ethic?

Are you satisfied with your personal inventory?

Fulfilling the Contract

Now that your personal inventory is complete, it is appropriate to look at your professional inventory. Look at the materials you collected at the beginning of the chapter. Consider your work performance now as if you are your supervisor. What were your expectations when you completed the exercise in chapter 1 about developing your contract? Did all your expectations get written into this semester's field contract? If not, do you still need to learn those specific tasks? How are the essential roles that you need to learn as a generalist social work practitioner working out in this agency? Your evaluation should take all these items into account and try to accurately reflect what you have done, how you did it, and what you should do next.

Your contract with the agency is an agreement between two parties. You agreed to certain activities that you have knowledge about but no practical experience in. The agency has social work tasks to give you practical experience and supervision. Select the tasks and objectively examine your completion and mastery of them. For instance, maybe one of the tasks in your learning contract was to facilitate a group. Ask yourself these questions.

Have I facilitated a group yet?

How often? How did I do?

Am I comfortable facilitating a group?

Have I dealt with the behavioral challenges that have occurred in group?

Did I start the group on time?

Did I use the time well, being prepared with enough material that is appropriate for the populations that I was working with?

Most importantly, did I put my best effort into this specific component of the contract?

These are the types of questions you need to ask for every item of your contract. Once you have completed each item of the contract, give your overall impressions of your work at the internship this semester. Rate yourself on the questions in table 14.1.

Table 14.1

	Needs immediate attention	Poor	Adequate	Good	No need for improvement
	1	2	3	4	5
How was your overall performance?					
Do you have the potential to be an effective social worker?					
Are your values consistent with social work?					
Is this the population you would consider working with?					
Is social work the field for you?					

Developing a New Contract

When you have completed this evaluation, think about next semester and developing a new contract. Questions to ask yourself include

What areas of this semester's contract still need improvement or refinement?

What areas of this semester's contact were not started, because of the needs of the agency?

What do I want to learn that I have not been exposed to?

What things on the contract do I think I can do independently and would like to continue to do?

Is there an area of course work that I have not yet integrated into my internship and that I need help learning how to apply (a particular theory or skill)?

Is there anything else I want to include for my personal development or knowledge?

You have just established your new learning goals for your professional development next semester. It is time to set up a meeting with your supervisor to discuss these items, your evaluation, and your new contract for next semester. You should let your supervisor know that you want to discuss all this when you set up the meeting. That gives him or her time to prepare for the meeting as well.

The NASW Code of Ethics covers evaluation from the perspectives of both students and employees. Section 3.02b states, "Social workers who function as educators or field instructors for students should evaluate students' performance in a manner that is fair and respectful." Further on, section 3.03 speaks to evaluation of employees: "Social workers who have responsibility for evaluating the performance of others should fulfill such responsibility in a fair and considerate manner and on the basis of clearly stated criteria."

In the meeting with your supervisor, a variety of outcomes are possible. The easiest is that you and your supervisor agree on the goals that you have achieved and the areas where you need to grow. That is the best possible scenario. You should be prepared for the more common situation, however, where you don't see eye to eye on every item of the contract. Your supervisor could evaluate you higher than you evaluate yourself, or you might evaluate yourself higher than your supervisor does.

If your supervisor sees you as a much stronger student than you have given yourself credit for, one agenda item for supervision is your self-perception. Why do you expect so much from yourself, why are you so critical of yourself, and why is your self-confidence not yet fully developed, are all questions that need to be explored. When you get insight into this issue and work on it, usually it is beneficial in your professional and personal life. These questions, of course, assume that you were not just downplaying your answers to please your supervisor.

The other scenario, your rating yourself higher than your supervisor does, happens much less often than the other two possibilities. The reasons for your difference of opinion may be limited insight about how others perceive you, an unclear expectation, miscommunication, lack of supervision, and a personality conflict. Regardless of the reason, this evaluation will be unpleasant for you to sit through. It is important that you receive this feedback in a nondefensive manner, hoping that it will improve your performance as a social work intern. Our hope is that this information is not new to you, and that you and your supervisor have spoken about these areas prior to the formal evaluation. If that's the case, you shouldn't be shocked, but it always looks worse on paper.

It is important to assess the reason for discrepancy between your thoughts about the evaluation and your supervisor's thoughts. The reason will help you proceed with the feedback. If you had no idea that you were being perceived in a certain way, we suggest you get a reality check by talking to your field coordinator, your field instructor, and your adviser, and perhaps family, friends, and former employers. They might be able to present the information so that you can learn from it and determine why your perception is a problem.

For instance, because of your personality you may not like to sit through meetings where things are discussed for a long time, you may be avoiding frustration by not focusing fully on the discussion. Your supervisor may consider that an uncaring attitude and lack of concentration. You may not understand that, but with a teacher's help you may be able to see how that particular mannerism may come across differently than intended. You may understand the need to change your behavior, even if you can't change your personality and the meetings are still difficult to sit through. If the problem ends up being about unclear expectations or miscommunications, you need to work really hard next semester toward being open to feedback (without being defensive). Work on communicating clearly how you feel and ask a lot of questions to be sure you and your supervisor understand the same thing. Often field supervisors expect interns to be self-starters and people who initiate their own tasks, when you thought you should be waiting for direction. Be clear about what the agency expects.

If the issue is about personality or lack of supervision, you will need to discuss your thoughts and feelings with your supervisor. Please be sure that you are tactful and diplomatic but also assertive. This may include writing on your evaluation that you don't agree with all parts of the evaluation, and asking that the evaluation that you prepared be attached to the document your supervisor created.

This piece of development (doing separate evaluations) is extremely important for you as a professional social worker. It is great if both of you agree on your performance and it was a good evaluation. But if anything else happens, you have a unique learning opportunity. You can learn how to make a more complete appraisal, comparing yourself to where you started when you joined the field, or you can learn how to negotiate, accept constructive criticism, advocate for yourself, and how to work with someone in an awkward and difficult situation.

Let us detour for a second on this important point. As you enter the professional world, recognize that you won't like everyone that you work with. Sometimes you won't get along with everyone you work with, including your supervisor. This in itself is not a good reason to leave a job. You have to take into consideration your responsibility to your clients or the program you are working on. Clients have the right to services and some consistency in a social worker. You have to consider your own marketability. Soon you will no longer be a student who can work one place for a semester and change jobs without consequences. You are now a professional, and your next employer will be wondering why you change jobs so frequently. For your own benefit, you need to stay at a job for at least a year. Learning how to deal with a difficult relationship with your supervisor will be your challenge while you also complete your job functions. Trust us when we say that in the long run you will benefit from this tremendously. It will be important to hear your supervisor's feedback and let him or her know, in a very professional way, with respect toward the position in the agency, why you disagree. Remain composed and level but express your opinion as clearly as possible.

Back to the evaluation and negotiation of the second-semester learning contract: if the evaluation does not go well, you can ask that the renegotiation of your next semester contract be postponed. You can say that you want to use the time to take into account your supervisor's comments and revise the contract. This gives you time to get some feedback from others and figure out what you want to say to your supervisor. Based upon that information, you may want to change your learning contract for next semester.

In rare instances your field placement may be changed if your school official (field coordinator and/or field instructor) decides that the relationship between you and your supervisor won't work. If that is the case, you will need to leave professionally and terminate responsibly (turn to the next chapter now). This situation could arise when your supervisor refuses to let you do some basic social work tasks on your own and you cannot get experience. Once we had a supervisor who went on maternity leave and the person covering for her believed social workers could only case manage. The supervisor would not let the intern cofacilitate groups, complete biopsychosocials, or develop treatment plans. That person's bias prevented a good learning environment for our student, and we found another field placement.

Although self-evaluation may be difficult for you at first, it is an excellent habit to get into both for your annual performance appraisal and for your own daily activities. During your daily activities you may not have the opportunity to process a session after it has occurred. But try to answer the questions in the box.

Self-supervision questions

Do I have all the information I need for this case?

Is there information missing, or am I assuming information that is not there?

Did I use the right approach with the client?

What is my next step?

Do I need to review or read about any new material before I see the client again?

Do I know how to access resources that my client may need?

What skills or tools do I need to hone before I work with this client again?

Was I culturally sensitive in my dealings with my client?

Was I ethical in my dealings with my client?

Do I know and understand my individual style yet?

What do I need to discuss in supervision about this case?

By the time you reach this chapter, your supervisor may have already completed your evaluation. That does not mean that you cannot evaluate yourself. We encourage you to give yourself an opportunity to complete the evaluation. If there is disparity, ask yourself why. If you need to have another conversation with your supervisor, ask for one and discuss the discrepancies. If you still disagree, ask for an addendum that you have written, explaining your opinion of the evaluation.

We wish you luck with this process. It takes training, discipline, and objectivity to accurately evaluate your own social work practice. Yet it is an important component of developing a professional and personal inventory that will build character and responsibility.

Integration of other course material

HBSE	What do you think about the assessment process that you have employed with your clients thus far? What can be added or deleted from the process?
Policy	What does the law say about your need for continuing evaluation and education?
Practice	What can you do to evaluate your practice with clients?
Research	What are ways that you can evaluate your practice with clients?

Resources

Self-evaluation
http://www.joe.org/joe/1999april/tt1.html

Field evaluation forms
http://bluehawk.monmouth.edu/socialwork/Main_SW.html

Revise your learning contract. Answer these questions. Take your notes with you when you sit down with your supervisor to discuss your second-semester learning contract.

What haven't I experienced at my internship that I still hope to experience?

What specific knowledge do I still need to be exposed to?

What specific skills or techniques do I need to sharpen?

How should supervision change for the next semester?

Do I have the ability to work independently, or do I need more experience working with close supervision?

Where do I stand in terms of my commitment to the agency? How are my hours? Have I experienced or seen all aspects of the agency and its services?

Are there other agency activities I want to be exposed to (e.g., budgeting, administration, board meetings, grant writing)?

Have I been exposed to collaborating agencies and learned about all the resources that the clients need to have access to?

Add other thoughts you have about your internship.

Chapter 15
Termination and Evaluation of Client Progress

It seems appropriate that the last chapter of the book should be about endings! Termination is probably one of the most important components of the social work relationship and may be one of the least well addressed areas of social work. That could be because it's an ending and many people are in a hurry to finish things or they do not like endings themselves. Those endings can be at the appropriate time (i.e., the client has successfully completed treatment) or premature because you or the client is leaving prior to successful completion. This chapter explains why termination is important and how to terminate successfully.

Termination

The easiest way to explain why termination is so important is to look at the case of a young child. Tyrone, an African American thirteen-year-old male, was left in a bus station by his mother when he was five. His mother took his two older sisters to the bathroom, and told him to stay right there and she would be right back. Two days later, a passenger waiting for a bus found him crying and huddled under a bench. (True story, the name was changed.) Tyrone became a ward of the state and by the age of thirteen had been removed from ten foster homes. He was removed from some homes because he tried to run away to find his mother, other homes because he got too big and the foster parents wanted little children, and the most recent move was because he was too angry and acted out often. By the time Tyrone came to the group home where he currently resides, he had had eleven sets of parents and six case workers from the county where he resided, all of whom worked for children's protective services. His mother still had legal custody because none of the workers took action to terminate parental rights. They had found Mom but had failed to develop a reunification plan that she abided by. Mom expressed interest in wanting Tyrone back.

Empathize for a moment. Wouldn't you be angry if you were Tyrone? He was all over the system with biological and foster parents and no consistency in case workers. Eventually, Tyrone was able to verbalize that he had no trust in anyone. Every time he trusted people, they left him, most of the time with no notice at all. Tyrone said that twice he was picked up at school and was told he would not be returning to his foster home. One time it was a new case worker who picked him up and told him his old worker had quit last month. Everyone left Tyrone, without notice or explanation. Even after sessions with the social worker, he could never trust that anyone would be there for him or that people wouldn't leave without saying good-bye.

The moral of this story is that termination should be done ethically and professionally for your benefit and for the benefit of your clients. Tyrone will eventually grow up to be an adult. To some of us, his story will be less traumatic because he will be older, and so much time will have elapsed between his traumatic childhood and his adulthood. Some people will figure he needs to get over it and see no connection to any issues he faces now and the lack of endings in his life. Think of Tyrone and every other client you have met thus far in your internship while we discuss termination.

When do you think the termination process begins? A week before a client leaves? A month? Two months? Actually, the termination process begins when the client arrives for intake. It is your goal from the beginning to have your client successfully complete your program. Even if your client is chronically mentally ill or developmentally disabled, your hope is he or she will do well enough in your program to live independently (if you are a group home), or attend fewer days (if you are a partial program or sheltered workshop). That being said, you take a biopsychosocial assessment, develop a treatment plan, and work on the goals that the client needs to achieve so that he or she no longer needs your services. When that day comes, it does not mean that you send your client off and say you are done, nor does it mean that your client has nothing else to work on.

Review of the Client's Progress

In the ideal world, you are constantly reviewing your client's treatment plan and revising it along the way. As you become aware that your client is completing the goals, you need to discuss progress and begin thinking about an appropriate time for discharge. Talking about it, planning for it, and discussing options make the ending of treatment real for both you and the client. It is an opportunity to discuss what the client's plans are after treatment and the feelings associated with ending a relationship. Remember when you started working with the client? You developed a rapport, you got to know him or her as an individual, and now you will put an end to the relationship in the same manner you spent time developing the relationship.

As you discuss termination, share with your clients your assessment of their progress, any memorable stories you have about them, and areas that you see they will need to work on for the future. When you start this process will depend on the types of clients you have (age, level of functioning) and how long they will stay in your program. Ask your supervisor for guidance within your agency.

Client Termination

Some agencies are very short-term (inpatient psychiatric, whose average length of stay is under a week). You may not need to work much on termination with these clients, except to go over what you worked on and their appointments for follow-up care. Some agencies offer longer treatment care where clients may live in the program for two years or longer (independent living, correctional facilities, and drug/alcohol rehabilitation programs). These clients will obviously have a stronger relationship with you, and the termination process will be longer and more detailed. Often the longer programs have formal graduations or terminations where everyone, residents and staff (clients and social workers), celebrates the accomplishment and come together to say good-bye.

The process described above works well if you are staying with the agency and the client is terminating successfully. Usually that means talking about growth while in treatment, what the client has accomplished, and what he or she needs to work on after leaving. If the client is going to another program, you will usually send paperwork summarizing treatment, but it is probably more important to have this conversation with clients.

At that point some clients may want to thank you for your help or give some feedback to you about the program. All of that is unsurprising and usual. Sometimes at this point, especially if you and a client got along very well, the client may ask permission to still call you, or ask you for your personal phone number. Clients, not totally inaccurately, think that now that they are not clients, you can have a personal relationship with them. You will need to explain that the boundary must remain in place in case they ever need your services again. The Code of Ethics is clear—once a client, always a client. If the client still wants to contact you at work, you will need to determine when he or she would want to do that and what your agency policy is. Many programs encourage clients to call when they are in trouble. One phone call could prevent a relapse or a readmission and be very beneficial. Other programs discourage former clients from calling because they do not have time to do the work required for the new clients, and no resources to offer the old clients. Find out what your agency policy is.

The other two ways termination occurs is when you the social worker (or intern) are leaving or when the client leaves prematurely. Many of you will leave your place of employment or your internship while in the middle of working with a client. Once you have decided to leave, or your internship hours are up, read your agency policy manual to determine if you need to give two weeks' notice or longer. Many of you may need to give one month's notice. The first person you will tell is your supervisor. Do *not* be tempted to tell your coworkers first. Nothing is more damaging than your supervisor finding out from someone else.

Once you tell your supervisor you are leaving, a few things need to be decided. First, you will establish your last day, how your responsibilities will be divided (including your clients), and in what order to tell people. Once you start telling people, everyone knows and will be talking. Don't wait long (more than a day) before starting to tell your clients. Depending on your agency and your relationships with your clients, you may tell them individually or you may tell them in a group. Remember the clients have to be served by the agency after you are gone, so if you are leaving because you dislike your supervisor or your agency, your clients do not need to know that. All you need to say is that you are moving on, when you are going, and that you wish them well. Some clients will be closer to you than others. Those who are closer to you are going to have a harder time; those who are not as close may not even care.

Some clients may need time to process your leaving and will want to speak to you later on or individually. That is one reason why you need to give them time to process and think. The two-week minimum is important. Clients who say you are critical to their treatment may begin to regress or act out, mostly because they are not sure how they will manage without you. If this part of the process is done properly, the client will not only survive the loss of you, but heal from other losses that were not resolved in the past. For some clients, this will take more than just one session. Reassure them that *they* made changes and that you were just guiding them, which is what the next worker will do.

If you are leaving because you don't like an agency, don't say anything bad, for your own sake. You don't want to burn your bridges. You never know when you may need assistance or when you may be working with some of the people in the agency again.

If the client is leaving before treatment is completed, it usually is because he or she is noncompliant, lacks funding, or is moving to another area. If the client is noncompliant or the program is out of funding, you need to be clear that the client still needs more treatment and refer him or her elsewhere, as the Code of Ethics indicates. If it is because the client is moving and you don't know the area to make a referral, you need to at minimum get phone numbers for the local mental health clinics and department of social services so the client has a lead on where to go. Ideally, you can find out more specific numbers than the client can. Just because the client's departure prompts the termination does not mean the termination process can't occur. Tell the client what he or she has completed and what areas still need work, and wish the client well.

When an appropriate amount of time is available a few things make the termination process very useful. You can update a client's ecomap and genogram with documentation in a one-page summary for the person who is taking over. This allows you and the client to recognize changes and gives the new social worker a brief synopsis of treatment issues to address. Ideally, discuss the history and treatment plan in a joint session with the client, yourself, and the new worker. The client hears what you are saying, adds any relevant material, and is part of the transition. He or she can see you passing the information on, and if the client's relationship is good with you, he or she will trust the person you are giving the case to. This makes the transition easier than if the client meets the person individually after you are gone.

The NASW Code of Ethics has a very detailed section on termination of services, section 1.16:

(a) Social workers should terminate services to clients and professional relationships with them when such services and relationships are no longer required or no longer serve the clients' needs or interests.

(b) Social workers should take reasonable steps to avoid abandoning clients who are still in need of services. Social workers should withdraw services precipitously only under unusual circumstances, giving careful consideration to all factors in the situation and taking care to minimize possible adverse effects. Social workers should assist in making appropriate arrangements for continuation of services when necessary.

(c) Social workers in fee-for-service settings may terminate services to clients who are not paying an overdue balance if the financial contractual arrangements have been made clear to the client, if the client does not pose an imminent danger to self or others, and if the clinical and other consequences of the current nonpayment have been addressed and discussed with the client.

(d) Social workers should not terminate services to pursue a social, financial, or sexual relationship with a client.

(e) Social workers who anticipate the termination or interruption of services to clients should notify clients promptly and seek the transfer, referral, or continuation of services in relation to the clients' needs and preferences.

(f) Social workers who are leaving an employment setting should inform clients of appropriate options for the continuation of services and of the benefits and risks of the options.

Coworkers and Supervisors

Up until now, we've just dealt with saying good-bye to clients. But you also have to terminate with your coworkers and supervisor. It is not uncommon to have a good-bye party, sometimes without clients, sometimes with them. Be prepared to say a few words and thank people who assisted you. Leaving coworkers is not the same as leaving clients. You can contact former coworkers. In fact, they become part of your network in your professional development and can be asked for information or resources whenever you think they may be helpful. Some of those relationships may continue as friendships after you no longer work at the agency. The good-bye process can be very draining and stressful.

Just because you are leaving does not mean that you don't have feelings for your clients, your coworkers, or your supervisor. Sometimes you need to move on for other reasons (like your internship is over), and it will be hard to leave. It is OK that people know that and for you to show your sadness (in an appropriate way).

As interns you hopefully have enjoyed your experience and learned a lot. Sometimes you like it so much that when you complete your hours you want to stay and volunteer. We want to caution you not to do that for a few reasons. First, it is valuable for you to learn how to terminate appropriately, especially if you have had losses in your life that you have not dealt with. Second, it's important early in your career to learn how to set up boundaries so you don't burn out. It is very easy to give a few hours here and a few hours there and suddenly be aware that you don't have time to breathe because you have overcommitted yourself. The third reason is that eventually, when you have your degree, agencies will need to compensate you for your time. Once you're established in your career, you may volunteer once again for other things, like your church, your local school system, or another nonrelated location. The last reason you should not stay on to work is that you need to finish the process you started, completing your degree and moving on to graduate school or employment in the field. Keep your focus: who knows, maybe your agency will even hire you when you graduate.

Miscellaneous Important Information

One last unrelated comment. If you are finishing this part of your internship in the fall, it is the beginning of the holiday season. This time is particularly difficult for our clients because of the termination issue. Many clients can't be with family during the holidays. All the messages on television, radio, and billboards are focused on giving gifts and being with family. If you were in a situation where you had no family (or could not be with them) and had no one giving you gifts, no one to give gifts to, and no one to spend the holidays with, how would you feel? Suicides increase during this time of year. Hospitalizations increase as does acting out. Be aware that this is a difficult time for most clients and you should have a little more patience and a whole lot more empathy. It will help the holidays go much more smoothly. As a new social worker, if you choose to work in a twenty-four-hour facility, be aware that you will probably be working at least one, and maybe more than one, holiday for a few years, at least until you get seniority. Plan activities that will be fun and healing for the clients. Also plan accordingly in your personal life, and if work disrupts your personal time, don't let clients know that you are upset about being there. At least you can celebrate later on or the next day with your family, whereas your clients cannot.

Conclusion

We would like to terminate appropriately by thanking you for being receptive to the activities in this book. We wish you all well in your journey to enter this profession that we care so deeply about. We are happy to have shared this part of the journey with you, and we invite you to use any of the activities you tried this semester with your clients and see how they respond!

Thoughts to ponder

How do you deal with saying good-bye to other people?

What are your thoughts as you think about leaving school and going into the workforce?

Can you think of situations where you experienced termination that left you feeling very upset? What could have been done differently?

Integration of other course material

HBSE	What HBSE content deals with endings? What do you know about client life stages and how clients handle endings?
Policy	What are the policies at your agency regarding termination with clients? Do these differ if you leave your job? Go on vacation? The client terminates first?
Practice	How have you experienced successful endings? What do you already do now to help your clients experience successful endings?
Research	What does the literature have to say about the termination process?

Resources

Women's business association on effective termination techniques
http://www.onlinewbc.gov/docs/manage/terminations.html

More about "Endings," from a social work perspective
http://www.ssw.pdx.edu/pgField_MoreAboutEndings.shtml

 **Green means go . . .**

Now that you have finished this semester of field, where do you want to go from here?

Appendix A
Code of Ethics of the National Association of Social Workers

Approved by the 1996 NASW Delegate Assembly and revised by the 1999 NASW Delegate Assembly

Preamble

The primary mission of the social work profession is to enhance human well-being and help meet the basic human needs of all people, with particular attention to the needs and empowerment of people who are vulnerable, oppressed, and living in poverty. A historic and defining feature of social work is the profession's focus on individual well-being in a social context and the well-being of society. Fundamental to social work is attention to the environmental forces that create, contribute to, and address problems in living.

Social workers promote social justice and social change with and on behalf of clients. "Clients" is used inclusively to refer to individuals, families, groups, organizations, and communities. Social workers are sensitive to cultural and ethnic diversity and strive to end discrimination, oppression, poverty, and other forms of social injustice. These activities may be in the form of direct practice, community organizing, supervision, consultation, administration, advocacy, social and political action, policy development and implementation, education, and research and evaluation. Social workers seek to enhance the capacity of people to address their own needs. Social workers also seek to promote the responsiveness of organizations, communities, and other social institutions to individuals' needs and social problems.

The mission of the social work profession is rooted in a set of core values. These core values, embraced by social workers throughout the profession's history, are the foundation of social work's unique purpose and perspective:

- service
- social justice
- dignity and worth of the person
- importance of human relationships
- integrity
- competence.

This constellation of core values reflects what is unique to the social work profession. Core values, and the principles that flow from them, must be balanced within the context and complexity of the human experience.

Purpose of the NASW Code of Ethics

Professional ethics are at the core of social work. The profession has an obligation to articulate its basic values, ethical principles, and ethical standards. The NASW Code of Ethics sets forth these values, principles, and standards to guide social workers' conduct. The Code is relevant to all social workers and social work students, regardless of their professional functions, the settings in which they work, or the populations they serve.

The NASW Code of Ethics serves six purposes:

1. The Code identifies core values on which social work's mission is based.

2. The Code summarizes broad ethical principles that reflect the profession's core values and establishes a set of specific ethical standards that should be used to guide social work practice.

3. The Code is designed to help social workers identify relevant considerations when professional obligations conflict or ethical uncertainties arise.

4. The Code provides ethical standards to which the general public can hold the social work profession accountable.

5. The Code socializes practitioners new to the field to social work's mission, values, ethical principles, and ethical standards.

6. The Code articulates standards that the social work profession itself can use to assess whether social workers have engaged in unethical conduct. NASW has formal procedures to adjudicate ethics complaints filed against its members.* In subscribing to this Code, social workers are required to cooperate in its implementation, participate in NASW adjudication proceedings, and abide by any NASW disciplinary rulings or sanctions based on it.

The Code offers a set of values, principles, and standards to guide decision making and conduct when ethical issues arise. It does not provide a set of rules that prescribe how social workers should act in all situations. Specific applications of the Code must take into account the context in which it is being considered and the possibility of conflicts among the Code's values, principles, and standards. Ethical responsibilities flow from all human relationships, from the personal and familial to the social and professional.

Further, the NASW Code of Ethics does not specify which values, principles, and standards are most important and ought to outweigh others in instances when they conflict. Reasonable differences of opinion can and do exist among social workers with respect to the ways in which values, ethical principles, and ethical standards should be rank ordered when they conflict. Ethical decision making in

---

*For information on NASW adjudication procedures, see NASW Procedures for the Adjudication of Grievances.

a given situation must apply the informed judgment of the individual social worker and should also consider how the issues would be judged in a peer review process where the ethical standards of the profession would be applied.

Ethical decision making is a process. There are many instances in social work where simple answers are not available to resolve complex ethical issues. Social workers should take into consideration all the values, principles, and standards in this Code that are relevant to any situation in which ethical judgment is warranted. Social workers' decisions and actions should be consistent with the spirit as well as the letter of this Code.

In addition to this Code, there are many other sources of information about ethical thinking that may be useful. Social workers should consider ethical theory and principles generally, social work theory and research, laws, regulations, agency policies, and other relevant codes of ethics, recognizing that among codes of ethics social workers should consider the NASW Code of Ethics as their primary source. Social workers also should be aware of the impact on ethical decision making of their clients' and their own personal values and cultural and religious beliefs and practices. They should be aware of any conflicts between personal and professional values and deal with them responsibly. For additional guidance social workers should consult the relevant literature on professional ethics and ethical decision making and seek appropriate consultation when faced with ethical dilemmas. This may involve consultation with an agency-based or social work organization's ethics committee, a regulatory body, knowledgeable colleagues, supervisors, or legal counsel.

Instances may arise when social workers' ethical obligations conflict with agency policies or relevant laws or regulations. When such conflicts occur, social workers must make a responsible effort to resolve the conflict in a manner that is consistent with the values, principles, and standards expressed in this Code. If a reasonable resolution of the conflict does not appear possible, social workers should seek proper consultation before making a decision.

The NASW Code of Ethics is to be used by NASW and by individuals, agencies, organizations, and bodies (such as licensing and regulatory boards, professional liability insurance providers, courts of law, agency boards of directors, government agencies, and other professional groups) that choose to adopt it or use it as a frame of reference. Violation of standards in this Code does not automatically imply legal liability or violation of the law. Such determination can only be made in the context of legal and judicial proceedings. Alleged violations of the Code would be subject to a peer review process. Such processes are generally separate from legal or administrative procedures and insulated from legal review or proceedings to allow the profession to counsel and discipline its own members.

A code of ethics cannot guarantee ethical behavior. Moreover, a code of ethics cannot resolve all ethical issues or disputes or capture the richness and complexity involved in striving to make responsible choices within a moral community. Rather, a code of ethics sets forth values, ethical principles, and ethical standards to which professionals aspire and by which their actions can be judged. Social workers' ethical behavior should result from their personal commitment to engage in ethical practice. The NASW Code of Ethics reflects the commitment of all social workers to uphold the profession's values and to act ethically. Principles and standards must be applied by individuals of good character who discern moral questions and, in good faith, seek to make reliable ethical judgments.

Ethical Principles

The following broad ethical principles are based on social work's core values of service, social justice, dignity and worth of the person, importance of human relationships, integrity, and competence. These principles set forth ideals to which all social workers should aspire.

Value: Service

Ethical Principle: Social workers' primary goal is to help people in need and to address social problems.

Social workers elevate service to others above self-interest. Social workers draw on their knowledge, values, and skills to help people in need and to address social problems. Social workers are encouraged to volunteer some portion of their professional skills with no expectation of significant financial return (pro bono service).

Value: Social Justice

Ethical Principle: Social workers challenge social injustice.

Social workers pursue social change, particularly with and on behalf of vulnerable and oppressed individuals and groups of people. Social workers' social change efforts are focused primarily on issues of poverty, unemployment, discrimination, and other forms of social injustice. These activities seek to promote sensitivity to and knowledge about oppression and cultural and ethnic diversity. Social workers strive to ensure access to needed information, services, and resources; equality of opportunity; and meaningful participation in decision making for all people.

Value: Dignity and Worth of the Person

Ethical Principle: Social workers respect the inherent dignity and worth of the person.

Social workers treat each person in a caring and respectful fashion, mindful of individual differences and cultural and ethnic diversity. Social workers promote clients' socially responsible self-determination. Social workers seek to enhance clients' capacity and opportunity to change and to address their own needs.

Social workers are cognizant of their dual responsibility to clients and to the broader society. They seek to resolve conflicts between clients' interests and the broader society's interests in a socially responsible manner consistent with the values, ethical principles, and ethical standards of the profession.

Value: Importance of Human Relationships

Ethical Principle: Social workers recognize the central importance of human relationships.

Social workers understand that relationships between and among people are an important vehicle for change. Social workers engage people as partners in the helping process. Social workers seek to strengthen relationships among people in a purposeful effort to promote, restore, maintain, and enhance the well-being of individuals, families, social groups, organizations, and communities.

Value: Integrity

Ethical Principle: Social workers behave in a trustworthy manner.

Social workers are continually aware of the profession's mission, values, ethical principles, and ethical standards and practice in a manner consistent with them. Social workers act honestly and responsibly and promote ethical practices on the part of the organizations with which they are affiliated.

Value: Competence

Ethical Principle: Social workers practice within their areas of competence and develop and enhance their professional expertise.

Social workers continually strive to increase their professional knowledge and skills and to apply them in practice. Social workers should aspire to contribute to the knowledge base of the profession.

Ethical Standards

The following ethical standards are relevant to the professional activities of all social workers. These standards concern (1) social workers' ethical responsibilities to clients, (2) social workers' ethical responsibilities to colleagues, (3) social workers' ethical responsibilities in practice settings, (4) social workers' ethical responsibilities as professionals, (5) social workers' ethical responsibilities to the social work profession, and (6) social workers' ethical responsibilities to the broader society.

Some of the standards that follow are enforceable guidelines for professional conduct, and some are aspirational. The extent to which each standard is enforceable is a matter of professional judgment to be exercised by those responsible for reviewing alleged violations of ethical standards.

1. Social Workers' Ethical Responsibilities to Clients

1.01 Commitment to Clients

Social workers' primary responsibility is to promote the well-being of clients. In general, clients' interests are primary. However, social workers' responsibility to the larger society or specific legal obligations may on limited occasions supersede the loyalty owed clients, and clients should be so advised. (Examples include when a social worker is required by law to report that a client has abused a child or has threatened to harm self or others.)

1.02 Self-Determination

Social workers respect and promote the right of clients to self-determination and assist clients in their efforts to identify and clarify their goals. Social workers may limit clients' right to self-determination when, in the social workers' professional judgment, clients' actions or potential actions pose a serious, foreseeable, and imminent risk to themselves or others.

1.03 Informed Consent

(a) Social workers should provide services to clients only in the context of a professional relationship based, when appropriate, on valid informed consent. Social workers should use clear and understandable language to inform clients of the purpose of the services, risks related to the services, limits to services because of the requirements of a third-party payer, relevant costs, reasonable alternatives, clients' right to refuse or withdraw consent, and the time frame covered by the consent. Social workers should provide clients with an opportunity to ask questions.

(b) In instances when clients are not literate or have difficulty understanding the primary language used in the practice setting, social workers should take steps to ensure clients' comprehension. This may include providing clients with a detailed verbal explanation or arranging for a qualified interpreter or translator whenever possible.

(c) In instances when clients lack the capacity to provide informed consent, social workers should protect clients' interests by seeking permission from an appropriate third party, informing clients consistent with the clients' level of understanding. In such instances social workers should seek to ensure that the third party acts in a manner consistent with clients' wishes and interests. Social workers should take reasonable steps to enhance such clients' ability to give informed consent.

(d) In instances when clients are receiving services involuntarily, social workers should provide information about the nature and extent of services and about the extent of clients' right to refuse service.

(e) Social workers who provide services via electronic media (such as computer, telephone, radio, and television) should inform recipients of the limitations and risks associated with such services.

(f) Social workers should obtain clients' informed consent before audiotaping or videotaping clients or permitting observation of services to clients by a third party.

1.04 Competence

(a) Social workers should provide services and represent themselves as competent only within the boundaries of their education, training, license, certification, consultation received, supervised experience, or other relevant professional experience.

(b) Social workers should provide services in substantive areas or use intervention techniques or approaches that are new to them only after engaging in appropriate study, training, consultation, and supervision from people who are competent in those interventions or techniques.

(c) When generally recognized standards do not exist with respect to an emerging area of practice, social workers should exercise careful judgment and take responsible steps (including appropriate education, research, training, consultation, and supervision) to ensure the competence of their work and to protect clients from harm.

1.05 Cultural Competence and Social Diversity

(a) Social workers should understand culture and its function in human behavior and society, recognizing the strengths that exist in all cultures.

(b) Social workers should have a knowledge base of their clients' cultures and be able to demonstrate competence in the provision of services that are sensitive to clients' cultures and to differences among people and cultural groups.

(c) Social workers should obtain education about and seek to understand the nature of social diversity and oppression with respect to race, ethnicity, national origin, color, sex, sexual orientation, age, marital status, political belief, religion, and mental or physical disability.

1.06 Conflicts of Interest

(a) Social workers should be alert to and avoid conflicts of interest that interfere with the exercise of professional discretion and impartial judgment. Social workers should inform clients when a real or potential conflict of interest arises and take reasonable steps to resolve the issue in a manner that makes the clients' interests primary and protects clients' interests to the greatest extent possible. In some cases, protecting clients' interests may require termination of the professional relationship with proper referral of the client.

(b) Social workers should not take unfair advantage of any professional relationship or exploit others to further their personal, religious, political, or business interests.

(c) Social workers should not engage in dual or multiple relationships with clients or former clients in which there is a risk of exploitation or potential harm to the client. In instances when dual or multiple relationships are unavoidable, social workers should take steps to protect clients and are responsible for setting clear, appropriate, and culturally sensitive boundaries. (Dual or multiple relationships occur when social workers relate to clients in more than one relationship, whether professional, social, or business. Dual or multiple relationships can occur simultaneously or consecutively.)

(d) When social workers provide services to two or more people who have a relationship with each other (for example, couples, family members), social workers should clarify with all parties which individuals will be considered clients and the nature of social workers' professional obligations to the various individuals who are receiving services. Social workers who anticipate a conflict of interest among the individuals receiving services or who anticipate having to perform in potentially conflicting roles (for example, when a social worker is asked to testify in a child custody dispute or divorce proceedings involving clients) should clarify their role with the parties involved and take appropriate action to minimize any conflict of interest.

1.07 Privacy and Confidentiality

(a) Social workers should respect clients' right to privacy. Social workers should not solicit private information from clients unless it is essential to providing services or conducting social work evaluation or research. Once private information is shared, standards of confidentiality apply.

(b) Social workers may disclose confidential information when appropriate with valid consent from a client or a person legally authorized to consent on behalf of a client.

(c) Social workers should protect the confidentiality of all information obtained in the course of professional service, except for compelling professional reasons. The general expectation that social workers will keep information confidential does not apply when disclosure is necessary to prevent serious, foreseeable, and imminent harm to a client or other identifiable person. In all instances, social workers should disclose the least amount of confidential information necessary to achieve the desired purpose; only information that is directly relevant to the purpose for which the disclosure is made should be revealed.

(d) Social workers should inform clients, to the extent possible, about the disclosure of confidential information and the potential consequences, when feasible before the disclosure is made. This applies whether social workers disclose confidential information on the basis of a legal requirement or client consent.

(e) Social workers should discuss with clients and other interested parties the nature of confidentiality and limitations of clients' right to confidentiality. Social workers should review with clients circumstances where confidential information may be requested and where disclosure of confidential information may be legally required.

This discussion should occur as soon as possible in the social worker–client relationship and as needed throughout the course of the relationship.

(f) When social workers provide counseling services to families, couples, or groups, social workers should seek agreement among the parties involved concerning each individual's right to confidentiality and obligation to preserve the confidentiality of information shared by others. Social workers should inform participants in family, couples, or group counseling that social workers cannot guarantee that all participants will honor such agreements.

(g) Social workers should inform clients involved in family, couples, marital, or group counseling of the social worker's, employer's, and agency's policy concerning the social worker's disclosure of confidential information among the parties involved in the counseling.

(h) Social workers should not disclose confidential information to third-party payers unless clients have authorized such disclosure.

(i) Social workers should not discuss confidential information in any setting unless privacy can be ensured. Social workers should not discuss confidential information in public or semipublic areas such as hallways, waiting rooms, elevators, and restaurants.

(j) Social workers should protect the confidentiality of clients during legal proceedings to the extent permitted by law. When a court of law or other legally authorized body orders social workers to disclose confidential or privileged information without a client's consent and such disclosure could cause harm to the client, social workers should request that the court withdraw the order or limit the order as narrowly as possible or maintain the records under seal, unavailable for public inspection.

(k) Social workers should protect the confidentiality of clients when responding to requests from members of the media.

(l) Social workers should protect the confidentiality of clients' written and electronic records and other sensitive information. Social workers should take reasonable steps to ensure that clients' records are stored in a secure location and that clients' records are not available to others who are not authorized to have access.

(m) Social workers should take precautions to ensure and maintain the confidentiality of information transmitted to other parties through the use of computers, electronic mail, facsimile machines, telephones and telephone answering machines, and other electronic or computer technology. Disclosure of identifying information should be avoided whenever possible.

(n) Social workers should transfer or dispose of clients' records in a manner that protects clients' confidentiality and is consistent with state statutes governing records and social work licensure.

(o) Social workers should take reasonable precautions to protect client confidentiality in the event of the social worker's termination of practice, incapacitation, or death.

(p) Social workers should not disclose identifying information when discussing clients for teaching or training purposes unless the client has consented to disclosure of confidential information.

(q) Social workers should not disclose identifying information when discussing clients with consultants unless the client has consented to disclosure of confidential information or there is a compelling need for such disclosure.

(r) Social workers should protect the confidentiality of deceased clients consistent with the preceding standards.

1.08 Access to Records

(a) Social workers should provide clients with reasonable access to records concerning the clients. Social workers who are concerned that clients' access to their records could cause serious misunderstanding or harm to the client should provide assistance in interpreting the records and consultation with the client regarding the records. Social workers should limit clients' access to their records, or portions of their records, only in exceptional circumstances when there is compelling evidence that such access would cause serious harm to the client. Both clients' requests and the rationale for withholding some or all of the record should be documented in clients' files.

(b) When providing clients with access to their records, social workers should take steps to protect the confidentiality of other individuals identified or discussed in such records.

1.09 Sexual Relationships

(a) Social workers should under no circumstances engage in sexual activities or sexual contact with current clients, whether such contact is consensual or forced.

(b) Social workers should not engage in sexual activities or sexual contact with clients' relatives or other individuals with whom clients maintain a close personal relationship when there is a risk of exploitation or potential harm to the client. Sexual activity or sexual contact with clients' relatives or other individuals with whom clients maintain a personal relationship has the potential to be harmful to the client and may make it difficult for the social worker and client to maintain appropriate professional boundaries. Social workers—not their clients, their clients' relatives, or other individuals with whom the client maintains a personal relationship—assume the full burden for setting clear, appropriate, and culturally sensitive boundaries.

(c) Social workers should not engage in sexual activities or sexual contact with former clients because of the potential for harm to the client. If social workers engage in conduct contrary to this prohibition or claim that an exception to this prohibition is warranted because of extraordinary circumstances, it is social workers—not their clients—who assume the full burden of demonstrating that the former client has not been exploited, coerced, or manipulated, intentionally or unintentionally.

(d) Social workers should not provide clinical services to individuals with whom they have had a prior sexual relationship. Providing clinical services to a former sexual partner has the potential to be harmful to the individual and is likely to make it difficult for the social worker and individual to maintain appropriate professional boundaries.

1.10 Physical Contact

Social workers should not engage in physical contact with clients when there is a possibility of psychological harm to the client as a result of the contact (such as cradling or caressing clients). Social workers who engage in appropriate physical contact with clients are responsible for setting clear, appropriate, and culturally sensitive boundaries that govern such physical contact.

1.11 Sexual Harassment

Social workers should not sexually harass clients. Sexual harassment includes sexual advances, sexual solicitation, requests for sexual favors, and other verbal or physical conduct of a sexual nature.

1.12 Derogatory Language

Social workers should not use derogatory language in their written or verbal communications to or about clients. Social workers should use accurate and respectful language in all communications to and about clients.

1.13 Payment for Services

(a) When setting fees, social workers should ensure that the fees are fair, reasonable, and commensurate with the services performed. Consideration should be given to clients' ability to pay.

(b) Social workers should avoid accepting goods or services from clients as payment for professional services. Bartering arrangements, particularly involving services, create the potential for conflicts of interest, exploitation, and inappropriate boundaries in social workers' relationships with clients. Social workers should explore and may participate in bartering only in very limited circumstances when it can be demonstrated that such arrangements are an accepted practice among professionals in the local community, considered to be essential for the provision of services, negotiated without coercion, and entered into at the client's initiative and with the client's informed consent. Social workers who accept goods or services from clients as payment for professional services assume the full burden of demonstrating that this arrangement will not be detrimental to the client or the professional relationship.

(c) Social workers should not solicit a private fee or other remuneration for providing services to clients who are entitled to such available services through the social workers' employer or agency.

1.14 Clients Who Lack Decision-Making Capacity

When social workers act on behalf of clients who lack the capacity to make informed decisions, social workers should take reasonable steps to safeguard the interests and rights of those clients.

1.15 Interruption of Services

Social workers should make reasonable efforts to ensure continuity of services in the event that services are interrupted by factors such as unavailability, relocation, illness, disability, or death.

1.16 Termination of Services

(a) Social workers should terminate services to clients and professional relationships with them when such services and relationships are no longer required or no longer serve the clients' needs or interests.

(b) Social workers should take reasonable steps to avoid abandoning clients who are still in need of services. Social workers should withdraw services precipitously only under unusual circumstances, giving careful consideration to all factors in the situation and taking care to minimize possible adverse effects. Social workers should assist in making appropriate arrangements for continuation of services when necessary.

(c) Social workers in fee-for-service settings may terminate services to clients who are not paying an overdue balance if the financial contractual arrangements have been made clear to the client, if the client does not pose an imminent danger to self or others, and if the clinical and other consequences of the current nonpayment have been addressed and discussed with the client.

(d) Social workers should not terminate services to pursue a social, financial, or sexual relationship with a client.

(e) Social workers who anticipate the termination or interruption of services to clients should notify clients promptly and seek the transfer, referral, or continuation of services in relation to the clients' needs and preferences.

(f) Social workers who are leaving an employment setting should inform clients of appropriate options for the continuation of services and of the benefits and risks of the options.

2. Social Workers' Ethical Responsibilities to Colleagues

2.01 Respect

(a) Social workers should treat colleagues with respect and should represent accurately and fairly the qualifications, views, and obligations of colleagues.

(b) Social workers should avoid unwarranted negative criticism of colleagues in communications with clients or with other professionals. Unwarranted negative criticism may include demeaning comments that refer to colleagues' level of competence or to individuals' attributes such as race, ethnicity, national origin, color, sex, sexual orientation, age, marital status, political belief, religion, and mental or physical disability.

(c) Social workers should cooperate with social work colleagues and with colleagues of other professions when such cooperation serves the well-being of clients.

2.02 Confidentiality

Social workers should respect confidential information shared by colleagues in the course of their professional relationships and transactions. Social workers should ensure that such colleagues understand social workers' obligation to respect confidentiality and any exceptions related to it.

2.03 Interdisciplinary Collaboration

(a) Social workers who are members of an interdisciplinary team should participate in and contribute to decisions that affect the well-being of clients by drawing on the perspectives, values, and experiences of the social work profession. Professional and ethical obligations of the interdisciplinary team as a whole and of its individual members should be clearly established.

(b) Social workers for whom a team decision raises ethical concerns should attempt to resolve the disagreement through appropriate channels. If the disagreement cannot be resolved, social workers should pursue other avenues to address their concerns consistent with client well-being.

2.04 Disputes Involving Colleagues

(a) Social workers should not take advantage of a dispute between a colleague and an employer to obtain a position or otherwise advance the social workers' own interests.

(b) Social workers should not exploit clients in disputes with colleagues or engage clients in any inappropriate discussion of conflicts between social workers and their colleagues.

2.05 Consultation

(a) Social workers should seek the advice and counsel of colleagues whenever such consultation is in the best interests of clients.

(b) Social workers should keep themselves informed about colleagues' areas of expertise and competencies. Social workers should seek consultation only from colleagues who have demonstrated knowledge, expertise, and competence related to the subject of the consultation.

(c) When consulting with colleagues about clients, social workers should disclose the least amount of information necessary to achieve the purposes of the consultation.

2.06 Referral for Services

(a) Social workers should refer clients to other professionals when the other professionals' specialized knowledge or expertise is needed to serve clients fully or when social workers believe that they are not being effective or making reasonable progress with clients and that additional service is required.

(b) Social workers who refer clients to other professionals should take appropriate steps to facilitate an orderly transfer of responsibility. Social workers who refer clients to other professionals should disclose, with clients' consent, all pertinent information to the new service providers.

(c) Social workers are prohibited from giving or receiving payment for a referral when no professional service is provided by the referring social worker.

2.07 Sexual Relationships

(a) Social workers who function as supervisors or educators should not engage in sexual activities or contact with supervisees, students, trainees, or other colleagues over whom they exercise professional authority.

(b) Social workers should avoid engaging in sexual relationships with colleagues when there is potential for a conflict of interest. Social workers who become involved in, or anticipate becoming involved in, a sexual relationship with a colleague have a duty to transfer professional responsibilities, when necessary, to avoid a conflict of interest.

2.08 Sexual Harassment

Social workers should not sexually harass supervisees, students, trainees, or colleagues. Sexual harassment includes sexual advances, sexual solicitation, requests for sexual favors, and other verbal or physical conduct of a sexual nature.

2.09 Impairment of Colleagues

(a) Social workers who have direct knowledge of a social work colleague's impairment that is due to personal problems, psychosocial distress, substance abuse, or mental health difficulties and that interferes with practice effectiveness should consult with that colleague when feasible and assist the colleague in taking remedial action.

(b) Social workers who believe that a social work colleague's impairment interferes with practice effectiveness and that the colleague has not taken adequate steps to address the impairment should take action through appropriate channels established by employers, agencies, NASW, licensing and regulatory bodies, and other professional organizations.

2.10 Incompetence of Colleagues

(a) Social workers who have direct knowledge of a social work colleague's incompetence should consult with that colleague when feasible and assist the colleague in taking remedial action.

(b) Social workers who believe that a social work colleague is incompetent and has not taken adequate steps to address the incompetence should take action through appropriate channels established by employers, agencies, NASW, licensing and regulatory bodies, and other professional organizations.

2.11 Unethical Conduct of Colleagues

(a) Social workers should take adequate measures to discourage, prevent, expose, and correct the unethical conduct of colleagues.

(b) Social workers should be knowledgeable about established policies and procedures for handling concerns about colleagues' unethical behavior. Social workers should be familiar with national, state, and local procedures for handling ethics complaints. These include policies and procedures created by NASW, licensing and regulatory bodies, employers, agencies, and other professional organizations.

(c) Social workers who believe that a colleague has acted unethically should seek resolution by discussing their concerns with the colleague when feasible and when such discussion is likely to be productive.

(d) When necessary, social workers who believe that a colleague has acted unethically should take action through appropriate formal channels (such as contacting a state licensing board or regulatory body, an NASW committee on inquiry, or other professional ethics committees).

(e) Social workers should defend and assist colleagues who are unjustly charged with unethical conduct.

3. Social Workers' Ethical Responsibilities in Practice Settings

3.01 Supervision and Consultation

(a) Social workers who provide supervision or consultation should have the necessary knowledge and skill to supervise or consult appropriately and should do so only within their areas of knowledge and competence.

(b) Social workers who provide supervision or consultation are responsible for setting clear, appropriate, and culturally sensitive boundaries.

(c) Social workers should not engage in any dual or multiple relationships with supervisees in which there is a risk of exploitation of or potential harm to the supervisee.

(d) Social workers who provide supervision should evaluate supervisees' performance in a manner that is fair and respectful.

3.02 Education and Training

(a) Social workers who function as educators, field instructors for students, or trainers should provide instruction only within their areas of knowledge and competence and should provide instruction based on the most current information and knowledge available in the profession.

(b) Social workers who function as educators or field instructors for students should evaluate students' performance in a manner that is fair and respectful.

(c) Social workers who function as educators or field instructors for students should take reasonable steps to ensure that clients are routinely informed when services are being provided by students.

(d) Social workers who function as educators or field instructors for students should not engage in any dual or multiple relationships with students in which there is a risk of exploitation or potential harm to the student. Social work educators and field instructors are responsible for setting clear, appropriate, and culturally sensitive boundaries.

3.03 Performance Evaluation

Social workers who have responsibility for evaluating the performance of others should fulfill such responsibility in a fair and considerate manner and on the basis of clearly stated criteria.

3.04 Client Records

(a) Social workers should take reasonable steps to ensure that documentation in records is accurate and reflects the services provided.

(b) Social workers should include sufficient and timely documentation in records to facilitate the delivery of services and to ensure continuity of services provided to clients in the future.

(c) Social workers' documentation should protect clients' privacy to the extent that is possible and appropriate and should include only information that is directly relevant to the delivery of services.

(d) Social workers should store records following the termination of services to ensure reasonable future access. Records should be maintained for the number of years required by state statutes or relevant contracts.

3.05 Billing

Social workers should establish and maintain billing practices that accurately reflect the nature and extent of services provided and that identify who provided the service in the practice setting.

3.06 Client Transfer

(a) When an individual who is receiving services from another agency or colleague contacts a social worker for services, the social worker should carefully consider the client's needs before agreeing to provide services. To minimize possible confusion and conflict, social workers should discuss with potential clients the nature of the clients' current relationship with other service providers and the implications, including possible benefits or risks, of entering into a relationship with a new service provider.

(b) If a new client has been served by another agency or colleague, social workers should discuss with the client whether consultation with the previous service provider is in the client's best interest.

3.07 Administration

(a) Social work administrators should advocate within and outside their agencies for adequate resources to meet clients' needs.

(b) Social workers should advocate for resource allocation procedures that are open and fair. When not all clients' needs can be met, an allocation procedure should be developed that is nondiscriminatory and based on appropriate and consistently applied principles.

(c) Social workers who are administrators should take reasonable steps to ensure that adequate agency or organizational resources are available to provide appropriate staff supervision.

(d) Social work administrators should take reasonable steps to ensure that the working environment for which they are responsible is consistent with and encourages compliance with the NASW Code of Ethics. Social work administrators should take reasonable steps to eliminate any conditions in their organizations that violate, interfere with, or discourage compliance with the Code.

3.08 Continuing Education and Staff Development

Social work administrators and supervisors should take reasonable steps to provide or arrange for continuing education and staff development for all staff for whom they are responsible. Continuing education and staff development should address current knowledge and emerging developments related to social work practice and ethics.

3.09 Commitments to Employers

(a) Social workers generally should adhere to commitments made to employers and employing organizations.

(b) Social workers should work to improve employing agencies' policies and procedures and the efficiency and effectiveness of their services.

(c) Social workers should take reasonable steps to ensure that employers are aware of social workers' ethical obligations as set forth in the NASW Code of Ethics and of the implications of those obligations for social work practice.

(d) Social workers should not allow an employing organization's policies, procedures, regulations, or administrative orders to interfere with their ethical practice of social work. Social workers should take reasonable steps to ensure that their employing organizations' practices are consistent with the NASW Code of Ethics.

(e) Social workers should act to prevent and eliminate discrimination in the employing organization's work assignments and in its employment policies and practices.

(f) Social workers should accept employment or arrange student field placements only in organizations that exercise fair personnel practices.

(g) Social workers should be diligent stewards of the resources of their employing organizations, wisely conserving funds where appropriate and never misappropriating funds or using them for unintended purposes.

3.10 Labor-Management Disputes

(a) Social workers may engage in organized action, including the formation of and participation in labor unions, to improve services to clients and working conditions.

(b) The actions of social workers who are involved in labor-management disputes, job actions, or labor strikes should be guided by the profession's values, ethical principles, and ethical standards. Reasonable differences of opinion exist among social workers concerning their primary obligation as professionals during an actual or threatened labor strike or job action. Social workers should carefully examine relevant issues and their possible impact on clients before deciding on a course of action.

4. Social Workers' Ethical Responsibilities as Professionals

4.01 Competence

(a) Social workers should accept responsibility or employment only on the basis of existing competence or the intention to acquire the necessary competence.

(b) Social workers should strive to become and remain proficient in professional practice and the performance of professional functions. Social workers should critically examine and keep current with emerging knowledge relevant to social work. Social workers should routinely review the professional literature and participate in continuing education relevant to social work practice and social work ethics.

(c) Social workers should base practice on recognized knowledge, including empirically based knowledge, relevant to social work and social work ethics.

4.02 Discrimination

Social workers should not practice, condone, facilitate, or collaborate with any form of discrimination on the basis of race, ethnicity, national origin, color, sex, sexual orientation, age, marital status, political belief, religion, or mental or physical disability.

4.03 Private Conduct

Social workers should not permit their private conduct to interfere with their ability to fulfill their professional responsibilities.

4.04 Dishonesty, Fraud, and Deception

Social workers should not participate in, condone, or be associated with dishonesty, fraud, or deception.

4.05 Impairment

(a) Social workers should not allow their own personal problems, psychosocial distress, legal problems, substance abuse, or mental health difficulties to interfere with their professional judgment and performance or to jeopardize the best interests of people for whom they have a professional responsibility.

(b) Social workers whose personal problems, psychosocial distress, legal problems, substance abuse, or mental health difficulties interfere with their professional judgment and performance should immediately seek consultation and take appropriate remedial action by seeking professional help, making adjustments in workload, terminating practice, or taking any other steps necessary to protect clients and others.

4.06 Misrepresentation

(a) Social workers should make clear distinctions between statements made and actions engaged in as a private individual and as a representative of the social work profession, a professional social work organization, or the social worker's employing agency.

(b) Social workers who speak on behalf of professional social work organizations should accurately represent the official and authorized positions of the organizations.

(c) Social workers should ensure that their representations to clients, agencies, and the public of professional qualifications, credentials, education, competence, affiliations, services provided, or results to be achieved are accurate. Social workers should claim only those relevant professional credentials they actually possess and take steps to correct any inaccuracies or misrepresentations of their credentials by others.

4.07 Solicitations

(a) Social workers should not engage in uninvited solicitation of potential clients who, because of their circumstances, are vulnerable to undue influence, manipulation, or coercion.

(b) Social workers should not engage in solicitation of testimonial endorsements (including solicitation of consent to use a client's prior statement as a testimonial endorsement) from current clients or from other people who, because of their particular circumstances, are vulnerable to undue influence.

4.08 Acknowledging Credit

(a) Social workers should take responsibility and credit, including authorship credit, only for work they have actually performed and to which they have contributed.

(b) Social workers should honestly acknowledge the work of and the contributions made by others.

5. Social Workers' Ethical Responsibilities to the Social Work Profession

5.01 Integrity of the Profession

(a) Social workers should work toward the maintenance and promotion of high standards of practice.

(b) Social workers should uphold and advance the values, ethics, knowledge, and mission of the profession. Social workers should protect, enhance, and improve the integrity of the profession through appropriate study and research, active discussion, and responsible criticism of the profession.

(c) Social workers should contribute time and professional expertise to activities that promote respect for the value, integrity, and competence of the social work profession. These activities may include teaching, research, consultation, service, legislative testimony, presentations in the community, and participation in their professional organizations.

(d) Social workers should contribute to the knowledge base of social work and share with colleagues their knowledge related to practice, research, and ethics. Social workers should seek to contribute to the profession's literature and to share their knowledge at professional meetings and conferences.

(e) Social workers should act to prevent the unauthorized and unqualified practice of social work.

5.02 Evaluation and Research

(a) Social workers should monitor and evaluate policies, the implementation of programs, and practice interventions.

(b) Social workers should promote and facilitate evaluation and research to contribute to the development of knowledge.

(c) Social workers should critically examine and keep current with emerging knowledge relevant to social work and fully use evaluation and research evidence in their professional practice.

(d) Social workers engaged in evaluation or research should carefully consider possible consequences and should follow guidelines developed for the protection of evaluation and research participants. Appropriate institutional review boards should be consulted.

(e) Social workers engaged in evaluation or research should obtain voluntary and written informed consent from participants, when appropriate, without any implied or actual deprivation or penalty for refusal to participate; without undue inducement to participate; and with due regard for participants' well-being, privacy, and dignity. Informed consent should include information about the nature, extent, and duration of the participation requested and disclosure of the risks and benefits of participation in the research.

(f) When evaluation or research participants are incapable of giving informed consent, social workers should provide an appropriate explanation to the participants, obtain the participants' assent to the extent they are able, and obtain written consent from an appropriate proxy.

(g) Social workers should never design or conduct evaluation or research that does not use consent procedures, such as certain forms of naturalistic observation and archival research, unless rigorous and responsible review of the research has found it to be justified because of its prospective scientific, educational, or applied value and unless equally effective alternative procedures that do not involve waiver of consent are not feasible.

(h) Social workers should inform participants of their right to withdraw from evaluation and research at any time without penalty.

(i) Social workers should take appropriate steps to ensure that participants in evaluation and research have access to appropriate supportive services.

(j) Social workers engaged in evaluation or research should protect participants from unwarranted physical or mental distress, harm, danger, or deprivation.

(k) Social workers engaged in the evaluation of services should discuss collected information only for professional purposes and only with people professionally concerned with this information.

(l) Social workers engaged in evaluation or research should ensure the anonymity or confidentiality of participants and of the data obtained from them. Social workers should inform participants of any limits of confidentiality, the measures that will be taken to ensure confidentiality, and when any records containing research data will be destroyed.

(m) Social workers who report evaluation and research results should protect participants' confidentiality by omitting identifying information unless proper consent has been obtained authorizing disclosure.

(n) Social workers should report evaluation and research findings accurately. They should not fabricate or falsify results and should take steps to correct any errors later found in published data using standard publication methods.

(o) Social workers engaged in evaluation or research should be alert to and avoid conflicts of interest and dual relationships with participants, should inform participants when a real or potential conflict of interest arises, and should take steps to resolve the issue in a manner that makes participants' interests primary.

(p) Social workers should educate themselves, their students, and their colleagues about responsible research practices.

6. Social Workers' Ethical Responsibilities to the Broader Society

6.01 Social Welfare

Social workers should promote the general welfare of society, from local to global levels, and the development of people, their communities, and their environments. Social workers should advocate for living conditions conducive to the fulfillment of basic human needs and should promote social, economic, political, and cultural values and institutions that are compatible with the realization of social justice.

6.02 Public Participation

Social workers should facilitate informed participation by the public in shaping social policies and institutions.

6.03 Public Emergencies

Social workers should provide appropriate professional services in public emergencies to the greatest extent possible.

6.04 Social and Political Action

(a) Social workers should engage in social and political action that seeks to ensure that all people have equal access to the resources, employment, services, and opportunities they require to meet their basic human needs and to develop fully. Social workers should be aware of the impact of the political arena on practice and should advocate for changes in policy and legislation to improve social conditions in order to meet basic human needs and promote social justice.

(b) Social workers should act to expand choice and opportunity for all people, with special regard for vulnerable, disadvantaged, oppressed, and exploited people and groups.

(c) Social workers should promote conditions that encourage respect for cultural and social diversity within the United States and globally. Social workers should promote policies and practices that demonstrate respect for difference, support the expansion of cultural knowledge and resources, advocate for programs and institutions that demonstrate cultural competence, and promote policies that safeguard the rights of and confirm equity and social justice for all people.

(d) Social workers should act to prevent and eliminate domination of, exploitation of, and discrimination against any person, group, or class on the basis of race, ethnicity, national origin, color, sex, sexual orientation, age, marital status, political belief, religion, or mental or physical disability.

Appendix B
Monmouth University

An Empowering, Strengths-Based Psychosocial Assement and Treatment Planning Outline for Practice with Families and Children

Identifying information
Reason for referral/presenting problem

  A. Referral source

  B. Summary of the presenting problem

  C. Impact of the presenting problem

Client and family description and functioning
Relevant History

  A. Family-of-origin history

  B. Relevant developmental history

  C. Family-of-creation history

  D. Educational and occupational history

  E. Religious (spiritual) development

  F. Social relationships

  G. Dating/marital/sexual relations

  H. Medical/psychological health

  I. Legal

  J. Environmental conditions

Workers' assessment

Treatment plan

Please see the following to guide your writing within each area.

Developed by Nora Smith and Irene Bush, Mommouth University, West Long Branch, NJ (Smith & Bush, 1998b).

Identifying Information

This section should include such information as age, sex, race, religion, marital status, occupation, living situation, and so on. Information should be factual, based on information from the client, collateral contacts, and case records.

Reason for Referral/Presenting Problem

This section should identify the referral source and give a summary of the reason for the referral. This should include the client's description of the problem or services needed, including the duration of the problem and its consequences for the client unit. Past intervention efforts by an agency or the individual and/or family related to the presenting problem should also be summarized.

In addition, comment on any of the following areas that have been *impacted* by the presenting problem:

- family situation
- physical and economic environment
- educational/occupational issues
- physical health
- relevant cultural, racial, religious, sexual orientation, and cohort factors
- current social/sexual/emotional relationships
- legal issues

Client and Family Description and Functioning

This section should contain data *observed* by the worker. Focusing on the first few interviews, include pertinent objective information about

- the client's physical appearance (dress, grooming, striking features);
- communication styles and abilities or deficits;
- thought processes (memory, intelligence, clarity of thought, mental status, etc.);
- expressive overt behaviors (mannerisms, speech patterns, etc.);
- reports from professionals or family (medical, psychological, legal); and
- mental status exam (if appropriate).

Relevant History

This section should discuss past history as it relates to the presenting problem. While this section should be as factual as possible, it is the place to present how the specifics of the client's culture, race, religion, or sexual orientation, for example, affect resolution of the presenting problem.

Include *applicable* information about each of the following major areas or about related areas relevant to your client. (You are not limited by the outline below.)

Family-of-Origin History. Family composition; birth order; where and with whom reared; relationship with parents or guardian; relationships with siblings; abuse or other trauma; significant family events (births, deaths, divorce, separations, moves, etc.) and their effect on the client(s).

Relevant Developmental History. Birth defects or problems around the birth process; developmental milestones including mobility (crawling, walking, coordination); speech; toilet training; eating or sleeping problems; developmental delays or gifted areas. This section is especially important for clients who are children. It is critical to identify nonwestern expectations and practices for child rearing and development for clients from diverse backgrounds. Nature of stressful experiences client has encountered throughout his or her life in relation to ability to handle them; how he or she has solved the "tasks" of various age levels.

Family-of-Creation History. Interacting roles within the family (e.g., who makes the decisions, handles the money, disciplines the children, does the marketing); typical family issues (e.g., disagreements, disappointments).

Educational and Occupational History. Level of education attained; school performance; learning problems, difficulties; areas of achievement; peer relationships. Skills and training; type of employment; employment history; adequacy of wage-earning ability; quality of work performance; relationship with authority figures and coworkers.

Religious (Spiritual) Development. Importance of religion in upbringing; affinity for religious or spiritual thought or activity; involvement in religious activities; positive or negative experiences.

Social Relationships. Size and quality of social network; ability to sustain friendships; pertinent social role losses or gains; social role performance within the client's cultural context. Patterns of familial and social relationships historically.

Dating/Marital/Sexual Relations. Type and quality of relationships; relevant sexual history; ability to sustain intimate (sexual and nonsexual) contact; significant losses; traumas; conflicts in intimate relationships; way of dealing with losses or conflicts. Currently, where do problems exist and where does the client manage successfully?

Medical/Psychological Health. Health problems, including drug, alcohol, or tobacco use or misuse; medications; accidents; disabilities; emotional difficulties including mental illness; psychological reports; hospitalizations; impact on functioning; use of previous counseling help.

Legal. Juvenile or adult contact with legal authorities; type of problem(s); jail or prison sentence; effects of rehabilitation.

Environmental Conditions. Urban or rural; indigenous or alien to the neighborhood where he or she lives; economic and class structure of the neighborhood in relation to that of the client; description of the home.

Worker's Assessment

This section should contain the thoughts and opinion of the treating social worker. It is based on initial observations and information-gathering efforts; however, it takes the observations and information to a new level. Here, the worker integrates his or her view with an understanding of the client's problem or situation, its underlying causes and/or contributing factors and the prognosis for change.

The worker summarizes his or her understanding of the client's presenting situation. To do this, he or she draws upon what is known about the current and past situation that has led to the presenting situation; the social, cultural, familial, psychological, and economic factors that contribute to creating the problem and/or support solutions to the problem. As appropriate, the worker comments on such factors as

- Social emotional functioning—ability to express feelings, ability to form relationships, predominant mood or emotional pattern (e.g., optimism, pessimism, anxiety, temperament, characteristic traits, overall role performance and social competence, motivation and commitment to treatment).

- Psychological factors—reality testing, impulse control, judgment, insight, memory or recall, coping style and problem-solving ability, characteristic defense mechanisms, notable problems. If applicable, include a formal diagnosis (e.g., DSM IV, Global Assessment Scale, etc.).

- Environmental issues and constraints or supports from the family, agency, community that affect the situation and its resolution. What does the environment offer for improved functioning (family, friends, church, school, work, clubs, groups, politics, and leisure-time activities).

- Issues related to cultural or other diversity that offer constraints or supports from the family, agency, community that affect the situation and its resolution.

- Strengths and weaknesses in relation to needs/demands/constraints in which he or she functions (ego functioning):
    capacities and skills
    activity patterns
    ways of communicating
    perceptions of him/herself and others
    how energy is invested
    what disturbs or satisfies him or her
    capacity for empathy and affection

affects and moods
control vs. impulsivity
spontaneity vs. inhibition
handling of sexuality and aggressiveness; dependency needs,
    self-esteem and anxiety
attitudes toward authority, peers, and others
nature of defenses
method and ability to solve problems

Conclude the assessment with a statement about the client's motivation for help, the agency's ability to provide help, and anticipated outcome of services to be provided.

Treatment Plan

This section should map out a realistic intervention strategy to address the range of problems and your assessment of the factors that underlie them. Your treatment plan should include:

- problem(s) chosen for intervention;

- goals and objectives;

- how the client, with the worker's help, will achieve these goals;

- the worker's role in the interventions;

- the anticipated time-frame (e.g., frequency of meetings, duration of the intervention);

- potential factors that may affect goal achievement (including client motivation; client willingness to take responsibility for change; client's personal and cultural resources; and/or personal abilities or limitations; agency resources or limitations; community resources of limitations); [and]

- method(s) by which goal achievement will be evaluated.

You may also wish to state whether further exploration is needed, whether you plan to refer the client to another agency or source of help instead of or in addition to your agency's help.

Appendix C
Monmouth University
Process Recording Outlines

Example 1

I. Preparation and Purpose—completed prior to contact with the client. Includes the following information: rationale for contact, relevant identifying information, prospective agenda, methods to be used, data to be obtained, preliminary assessment, issues for attention, and possible barriers.

II. Process Recording

Supervisory comments	Content-dialogue	Gut-level feelings

III. Plans—includes current and future plans

IV. Questions for Supervision

Developed by Nora Smith and Irene Bush, Mommouth University, West Long Branch, NJ (Smith & Bush, 1998a).

Monmouth University Process Recording Outlines

Example 2

I. Preparation and Purpose—completed prior to contact with the client. Includes the following information: rationale for contact, relevant identifying information, prospective agenda, methods to be used, data to be obtained, preliminary assessment, issues for attention, and possible barriers.

II. Observation

Summary of what occurred	Student thoughts and analysis, including interventions used

III. Plans—includes current and future plans

IV. Questions for Supervision

Developed by Nora Smith and Irene Bush, Mommouth University, West Long Branch, NJ (Smith & Bush, 1998a).

References

Barker, R. L. (1999). *The social work dictionary* (4th ed.). Washington, DC: NASW Press.

Conference of Intellectuals from Africa and Diaspora (CIAD). (1981, June). *African Charter on Human and People Rights*. Retrieved June 10, 2005, from http://africa-union.org

Congress, E. (1999). *Social work values and ethics: Identifying and resolving professional dilemmas*. New York: Wadsworth.

Goldstein, S. R., & Bebe, L. (1995). National Association of Social Workers. In R. Edwards (Ed.), *Encyclopedia of social work* (19th ed., Vol. 2, pp. 1747–1764). Washington, DC: NASW Press.

Luft, J. (1970). *Group process: An introduction to group dynamics* (2nd ed.). Palo Alto, CA: National Press.

Maslow, A. (1970). *Motivation and personality* (2nd ed.). New York: Harper and Row.

Smith, N., & Bush, I. (1998a). *Process recording examples*. West Long Branch, NJ: Monmouth University Department of Social Work.

Smith, N., & Bush, I. (1998b). *Psychosocial assessment and treatment planning outline: An empowering strengths-based approach*. West Long Branch, NJ: Monmouth University Department of Social Work.

United Nations. (1997, January). *Covenant on Civil and Political Rights*. Retrieved June 10, 2005, from United Nations site, http://hrweb.org/legal/cpr.html

Winston, C., & LeCroy, E. S. (2004). Public perception of social work: Is it what we think it is? *Social Work, 49*, 164–174.

Index

Notes